M000013394

OUTDOORS AUSTIN

A Sierra Club Guide

Third Edition

Austin Regional Group
of the
Sierra Club

Edited
by
Nancy Fuentes

For information, contact:
    Austin Sierra Club
    Attn: Book Committee
    P.O. Box 4581
    Austin, Texas 78765

ISBN 0-89096-693-1 (paperbound)

Library of Congress Catalog Card No. 94-66625

Outdoors Austin: A Sierra Club Guide is the
third edition of a book previously titled
Sierra Club Guide to Outdoors Austin,
which was last published in 1982.

SPONSORS

We wish to thank the organizations and businesses listed below for contributing toward the cost of producing this book. They are listed according to the size of their contributions, but all contributions, large and small, are greatly appreciated. Without them, this book would not have been possible.

Lower Colorado River Authority

IBM

Gage Furniture

Wilderness Supply

Whitewater Sports

Kestrel Printing

Victor Emmanuel

River Valley Resort

Rockin 'R' River Rides

Travel*Fest*

CONTENTS

ACKNOWLEDGMENTS

Warren Hancock, President of Wilderness Supply, planted the seed for this new edition of the book *Sierra Club Guide to Outdoors Austin* by encouraging the Austin Regional Group of the Sierra Club to update the book. He was the first to contribute financially to the effort. Nancy Fuentes assembled a committee of volunteers in the summer of 1992, the year the Sierra Club celebrated its centennial. One of the committee's goals was to improve the organization of the book so that information could be found more readily. Another goal was, of course, to update the book in light of Austin's growth over the last decade.

The following volunteers served on the book committee:

Sandra Bybee	Rebecca Patterson
Rebecca Davio	Philip Russell
Karen Fraser	Francis Seifert
Nancy Fuentes	Winnie M. Spitz
Mary Gow	Monica Walden
Ginny Johnson	Betty Walls
Jackie McFadden	George Zapalac

Rebecca Patterson contributed substantially to the effort by loaning her computer to Nancy Fuentes for an extended period of time. She deserves special commendation for her trust and generosity.

George Zapalac and Nancy Fuentes wrote Chapter 1, *In the Heart of the City,* and Chapter 2, *At the Park,* with help from Sandra Bybee and Karen Fraser. For Chapter 3, *On the Move,* Philip Russell wrote the sections on bicycling and caving, while Monica Walden wrote the camping and backpacking section and worked on the running section as well. For Chapter 4, *In and on the Water,* Sandra Bybee contributed material on swimming, Betty Walls wrote about canoeing, rafting, and tubing, and Francis Seifert prepared the section on sailing and windsurfing as well as the section on rocks and fossils for Chapter 7, *In Tune with Nature.* Ginny Johnson wrote the sections on archery, horseback riding, geology, and stargazing. The material on dog walks and on wildlife and rehabilitation for Chapter 6, *Out with Fauna and Friends,* was

written by Nancy Fuentes, as was Chapter 8, *For Special People.*
Winnie M. Spitz wrote Chapter 9, *Out for the View.*

Other sections of the book were farmed out to individuals not
actually on the committee. The book committee wishes to express
its appreciation to the people listed below for writing, revising, or
editing portions of the book.

George W. Batten III (rowing)
Mary Baughman (Texas Memorial Museum and moonlight towers)
Molly Bean (rock climbing)
Paul Breaux (stargazing)
Charles Chapman (rock climbing)
Carolyn Croom (Up in the Air)
Sam Fruehling (birdwatching)
Kimberly Geiser (wildflowers)
Steve Hanson (Wild Basin)
Lynette Holtz (gardens)
John Koepke (kayaking)
Gerry McNabb (nature photography)
Adam Metzger (rock climbing)
Dan Smith (birdwatching)
Art Souther (wildflowers)
Maynard Spitz (editing)
Gary Trommer (scuba diving)
Glenn Williams (running)
Merry Wolf (editing)

Several staff from the Austin Parks and Recreation Department,
including Jim Halbrook, Rosie Roegner, Sarah Macias, Stuart
Strong, and Donna Bohls, assisted with maps, photographs, and
editing. The *Austin American-Statesman* and its publication
entitled "This is Austin!" were good sources of information.

Monica Walden identified an artist and cartographer for the book.
The artist, John Dolley with The Graphic Eye, took care to produce
exactly the artwork we wanted. The cartographer, John Cotter with
Map Ventures, produced the maps. Karen Fraser built the database
needed for the index and geographic list of sites in the appendix.
Mary Gow worked on cover design and recruited Eric Beggs, who
provided the cover photographs.

The project was fortunate to have Monica Walden and Jackie

McFadden offering technical assistance and guidance during the book's development; their expertise and experience were invaluable. Jeanette Ivy donated typesetting and layout services that were a great help to Winnie M. Spitz, who assumed primary responsibility for final production of the book on the computer. Phoebe Allen, Molly Bean, Carolyn Croom, Karen Fraser, and Philip Russell all helped with the Index and the Geographic List of Sites. Dick Kallerman also assisted with the finishing touches during the final push to complete the book.

Rebecca Davio took the lead on fund-raising, getting help from Betty Walls and Nancy Fuentes. Rebecca Davio, Monica Walden, Sandra Bybee, Winnie M. Spitz, Ginny Johnson and her husband Les, and John Stolarek all assisted with seemingly small but critically important logistical tasks that keep a volunteer effort moving forward. At the "last minute," phone numbers, addresses, and directions were double-checked for accuracy by Carole Riley, Winnie M. Spitz, Vince Shouba, Linda Pulis, and Rebecca Patterson. Many corrections were made as a result of their efforts, but changes will inevitably occur after the printing of this book in spite of this last-minute check.

The book reflects our love for the outdoor resources around Austin. Our hope is that newcomers and old-timers alike will see and enjoy a part of Austin they might not otherwise have known had it not been for this book.

About This Guide

The area covered in this guide is roughly a circle around Austin with a radius of 100 miles. The circle extends out to Bastrop State Park to the east, Enchanted Rock State Natural Area to the west, and Guadalupe River State Park to the southwest. A map to use in conjunction with this book is:

■ *South Central Texas*, 4th ed. Pflugerville, Texas: Map Ventures, 1993.

This map was produced by John Cotter with Map Ventures. It shows the state parks and other sites in the area around Austin covered in the book. The Austin Parks and Recreation Department (PARD) from time to time produces a large facility locator map that shows where over 130 City of Austin parks and other resources are located. You are advised to contact PARD (499-6700) for this map or the best available materials that will substitute for it.

The Capitol of Texas Highway (Loop 360) and U.S. Highway 183 together form a loop or circle covering the central part of Austin. This central circle has 5 sectors bounded by major roadways as follows:

■ North: Loop 360, U.S. Highway 183, IH 35, and RM 2222

■ East: IH 35, U.S. Highway 183, and the Colorado River

■ Central: RM 2222, IH 35, the Colorado River, and a short stretch of Loop 360

■ South: the Colorado River, U.S. Highway 183, Ben White Boulevard (Texas Highway 71) , and Loop 1 (MoPac)

■ West: Loop 1 (MoPac), Loop 360, and the Colorado River

Outside the central circle lie 4 quadrants: northwest, northeast, southeast, and southwest. The Colorado River divides north from south, while IH 35 divides east from west. So, for example, the southeast quadrant is the area outside the central circle that lies south of the river and east of IH 35. The resulting map was used to organize the Geographic List of Sites appendix.

A person who plans an outing usually has a particular activity in mind, such as hiking, biking, or canoeing, so this book is organized by activity. Since many outdoor areas are multifunctional, however, the same area may be mentioned under 2 or more different activities. To avoid too much repetition, the book has an appendix in addition to the Index, which gives the name, address, and other

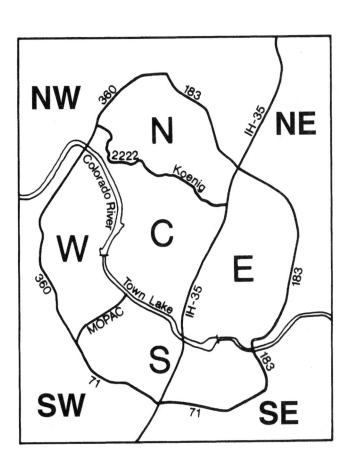

pertinent information for each site. The Geographic List of Sites is organized according to the scheme of sectors and quadrants described above. Another appendix lists resources for further information about Central Texas outdoor activities, including agencies, maps, and publications.

Many incorporated communities are adjacent to Austin, including Cedar Park, Jonestown, Lago Vista, Lakeway, Leander, Manor, Pflugerville, Rollingwood, Round Rock, San Leanna, Sunset Valley, and Westlake Hills. In general the outdoor resources in these areas are not covered in this book. If you live in one of these nearby cities, you may wish to contact your city's administrative office to inquire about outdoor recreation there.

Nor does the book attempt to cover comprehensively the cities of San Marcos, New Braunfels, and San Antonio (all south of Austin), although they offer some nice recreational opportunities. Driving south on IH 35 to San Marcos, you will find a visitor's center on the southbound access road of the highway (Exit 206). San Marcos is popular for **City Park** at the head of the San Marcos River and for **Aquarena Springs,** a marine amusement park famous for its underwater shows and glass-bottom boats. New Braunfels is known for its tubing on the **Comal River** and at **Schlitterbahn**, a water amusement park.

A notable spot in San Antonio is **Brackenridge Park**, the city's largest park, known for its zoo, the Sunken Gardens, and many other attractions. A rich source of information on San Antonio is the *Sierra Club Guide to Outdoor San Antonio and Vicinity,* prepared by the Alamo Regional Group of the Sierra Club. While New Braunfels, San Marcos, and San Antonio are not covered in detail here, it is good to know that these nearby cities have much to offer.

Many parks, pools, and other facilities charge entry fees, but since these are subject to change, they are not, as a rule, included in this book. You are advised to call ahead to determine not only entry fees but also user fees for campsites, cabins, screened shelters, or other park facilities. Reservations may be required, especially if you are planning an overnight stay. Information about park reservations appears at the end of Chapter 2, *At the Park.*

Chapters 3, 4, and 5 contain information about activities that can be risky or even dangerous, especially to the novice. Although words of caution, safety guidelines, and how-to publications appear in some sections of the book, they are by no means complete or comprehensive. The Sierra Club is not responsible for mishaps that may occur while engaging in activities described in this book. This book focuses on where to go and what to see. It is imperative that the reader be well informed of the risks associated with any sport and take precautions on an outing to ensure the safety of everyone involved.

We know that there are interesting natural places in and around Austin that have not found their way into this guide. If your favorite spot or activity is missing or if you know of changes, please mail the information to: Austin Sierra Club, Attn: Book Committee, P.O. Box 4581, Austin, Texas, 78765. We plan to update this book every few years. Your suggestions will be valuable grist for the mill.

We limited the scope of the book to activities consistent with the Sierra Club's philosophy: "to explore, enjoy, and protect the nation's scenic resources." We covered mainly recreational rather than competitive sports and omitted motorized sports, hunting, and fishing in the belief that it is best to enjoy an area in a quiet, natural way and to leave it in its natural state.

So if you want some good clean fun and healthful exercise, this book will give you some ideas, open some doors for you, or just kindle your interest in getting out there to enjoy Austin's beautiful outdoors.

OUTDOORS AUSTIN

INTRODUCTION

Lying along the Balcones Fault, Central Texas is a land of geological contrasts. To the west lies the Hill Country with its lakes, steep topography, and environmentally sensitive Edwards Aquifer. To the east lies flatter but greener pastoral countryside. Austin sits between the Balcones Escarpment and the Blackland Prairie, with IH 35 roughly dividing the two. Central Texas is home to a high number of rare species, including the Black-capped Vireo, Golden-cheeked Warbler, 5 cave invertebrates, and several plant species.

The 7 Highland Lakes of the Colorado River begin northwest of Austin and run in a southeast direction toward Austin, culminating in Town Lake. Every day runners and bicyclists enjoy the wonderful hike-and-bike trails around Town Lake, the center of outdoor activity downtown. On the south side of the lake are the city's "crown jewels"—Zilker Park, the Zilker Gardens, Barton Springs Pool, Barton Creek, and the Barton Creek Greenbelt. *Outside* magazine included Barton Springs and Barton Creek in a list of treasured urban places across the United States. Austinites have fought and won several hard political battles to preserve them.

Outdoor areas around Austin are managed by various agencies, although some areas are privately owned. A reasonably complete list of responsible public agencies is given below:

- Austin Parks and Recreation Department (PARD), 499-6700

- Lower Colorado River Authority (LCRA), Land Resources/Parks, 473-4083

- Texas Travel Information Center, Capitol Complex Visitor's Center, 463-8586

- Texas Parks and Wildlife Department (TPWD), Park/Camping Information, 389-8950 or 800/792-1112

- Travis County Parks, Visitors Information and Reservations, 473-9437

- University of Texas (UT), Recreational Sports, 471-1093

- U.S. Fish and Wildlife Service, 482-5700

Introduction

These agencies give out brochures, maps, and other publications about their facilities and programs. For maps of the hike-and-bike trails, for example, contact the Austin Parks and Recreation Department. Ask to be placed on PARD's mailing list to receive seasonal publications on outdoor nature activities, cultural arts, and other PARD programs. See *Agencies,* Appendix 2, for more information.

All phone numbers are area code 512 unless otherwise noted.

Whether you are a newcomer eager to learn what Austin has to offer, or a native looking for new, fresh places to see, this book is for you. Whether you prefer easy, moderate, or strenuous activities, you will find many activities in this book to help you enjoy the beautiful outdoors.

IN THE HEART OF THE CITY

Town Lake

Where the city straddles the Colorado River, 2 dams mark the upstream and downstream ends of Town Lake, the focus of outdoor activity in downtown Austin. **Town Lake Metropolitan Park** stretches along the banks of the Colorado River from Tom Miller Dam on the west to Colorado River Park on the east. This giant park contains 10.1 miles of jogging and bicycle trails (see *Hike-and-Bike Trails* later in this chapter). For the athlete, Town Lake Park boasts 17 ballfields for baseball, football, soccer and rugby, and volleyball. The area on the south side of Town Lake from Lamar Boulevard east to South First Street is known as **Auditorium Shores**, and many concerts and large events are held there. **Butler Shores** refers to that stretch of Town Lake from the Lamar bridge over the Colorado River to the east bank of Barton Creek. East of IH 35 favorite spots for large Town Lake gatherings are **Fiesta Gardens** and **Festival Beach**, which stretches from IH 35 east to Canadian Street. All along Town Lake, people flock to the hike-and-bike trails to walk, jog, bicycle, or otherwise enjoy the beauty of the Colorado River.

On the north side of the river people typically congregate where Austin High School, the Austin tennis courts, and a foot bridge over the river are all located together just east of where Loop 1 (MoPac) crosses the Colorado. You can get there from West Cesar Chavez but look carefully for signs telling you where to veer off and clover-leaf around to head south toward the high school. With plenty of space to park, many people begin and end their jaunt for the day here. A concrete gully, typically used as a boat launch, makes it an ideal spot to begin and end a canoe trip, too.

Just west of MoPac off Lake Austin Boulevard, one can turn south onto Deep Eddy Avenue to find one of the city's most popular swimming pools and parks. **Deep Eddy Pool** (472-8546), which is quite large, has a shallow end that is wonderful for children plus lanes at the other end for serious swimming. Pool hours depend on the time of year, so call ahead to find out when the pool is open. Next to Deep Eddy Pool is **Eilers Park**, complete with picnic tables, a playground, a sand court, and even an outdoor shower for cooling off after running the hike-and-bike trail that ends at the park.

Two scenic lookout points not to be missed on the south side of the river are the **gazebo** at Auditorium Shores and **Lou Neff Point** where the mouth of Barton Creek flows into the Colorado River. (See Chapter 9, *Out for the View*, for more information on views in this area.)

A bit farther up Barton Creek, Zilker Park Boat Rentals (478-3852) rents canoes. Not only canoe but also kayak rentals and lessons are available from Austin Canoe and Kayak (719-4386). On a beautiful day, many people canoe and row along these peaceful shores.

Speaking of canoes, it is an easy stretch to paddle upstream from the mouth of Barton Creek to **Red Bud Isle** just below Tom Miller Dam. Stop for a picnic on this little island and then paddle easily downstream back to where you started.

Besides enjoying the outdoors, Austinites participate actively in preserving it. Town Lake cleanups are organized periodically by the Texas General Land Office in cooperation with other sponsors, such as Keep Austin Beautiful, the City of Austin, and private corporations. At various points along the lake you can pick up litter and enjoy the outdoors at the same time, but wear shoes and gloves to protect yourself from broken glass and other sharp objects. At the end of the day volunteers celebrate with a party. For information call 800/85-BEACH or 499-2533.

■ Zilker Metropolitan Park and Barton Springs Pool

The heartbeat of Austin is **Zilker Metropolitan Park** (on Town Lake) 476-6922, commonly called Zilker Park for short but not to be confused with a very small park by that same name. The large park known as Zilker is "Austin's most beloved park," because of its beauty, many facilities, and central location on Barton Springs Road. A favorite part of the park is **Barton Springs Pool** (867-3080), a spring-fed pool that is nearly 1,000 feet long (see Chapter 4, *In and on the Water*, for more information on this pool). Baseball, football, soccer, and rugby fields welcome sport enthusiasts, while others enjoy the Botanical Gardens, the Austin Area Garden Center, and Zilker Hillside Theater. Children like the playscape near the pool, and they love to ride the *Zilker Eagle*, a miniature train that runs through the park. Special events like the annual Kite Contest in the spring attract crowds of adults and children alike, while the Zilker Clubhouse at the west end of the park is customarily used for smaller social functions.

Starting at the Barton Springs Pool bathhouse, the **Trail of Trees** helps you to identify 28 species of trees. A brochure is available from Parks and Recreational Department. In the **Austin Area Garden Center** on the north side of Barton Springs Road, you can enjoy an oriental garden with waterfalls and ponds, a rose garden, a butterfly trail, a xeriscape garden that demonstrates the principles of water conservation, and a small pioneer village.

Quite popular in the Zilker Botanical Gardens are the newly discovered **Zilker Dinosaur Trackways**. Dinosaur tracks believed to be those of an ostrich-like dinosaur, *ornithomimus,* were found in 1992. When these tracks were uncovered, bones of a marine turtle, *osteopygis*, were discovered as well. The estimated age of the tracks and bones is 100 million years, but ongoing research at the site will better determine information regarding the dinosaurs and their environment.

■ Austin Nature Center

At the west end of Zilker Park near MoPac, the **Austin Nature Center** (327-8180) is the focal point of the **Zilker Preserve**, where trails meander through 80 acres of woods, along a creek bed, and amid rock cliffs. Outdoors the wildlife exhibits of rehabilitated or orphaned animals, unable to return to the wild, are popular (injured or orphaned wild animals should be referred to Wildlife Rescue 472-WILD). The center also has indoor exhibits, including a hands-on Discovery Lab. The big event of the year is Safari, held the last weekend of April, but other activities scattered throughout the year include day camps for children, school programs, public programs, and teacher workshops. The center was featured in the March, 1993 issue of *Texas Parks and Wildlife.*

Hours are 9 a.m. to 5 p.m. Monday through Saturday and noon to 5 p.m. on Sunday. Take Barton Springs Road through Zilker Park, turn north onto Stratford Drive, and follow the signs to the parking area under the MoPac bridge. (See Chapter 9, *Out for the View*, for information on the Zilker Preserve Overlook.)

■ Greenbelts

Austin has over 2,000 acres of parkland along its rivers, creeks, and ravines through its system of greenbelts, open daily 5 a.m. to 10 p.m. The greenbelts are good for hiking, jogging, and in some areas rock climbing. Although not really suitable for touring bicycles, they are popular for mountain bikes. Hikers and mountain bikers should use the greenbelts only when the trails are dry to avoid eroding the trails, especially because little maintenance is provided to these natural areas.

The most popular greenbelt is the **Barton Creek Greenbelt** south of the Colorado River, which is 7.8 miles long and consists of 812 acres. This greenbelt extends upstream from Barton Springs Pool to Camp Craft Road. This is one of the most popular and interesting hiking experiences in Austin, particularly during the spring and early summer when the creek is flowing freely from rainfall runoff. During mid- and late summer, most of the runoff infiltrates rapidly through the streambed into the Edwards Aquifer, emerging at Barton Springs. Including the trailhead at Barton Springs Pool, there are 7 points of access to the greenbelt:

■ Zilker Park Trailhead Access, on the north side of Barton Springs Pool at the far west end of the parking lot

■ Spyglass Drive Access, where Spyglass Drive intersects with Barton Skyway on the north side of the creek near Campbell's Hole, a popular spot

■ Gus Fruh Park Access, at the far south end of Barton Hills Drive

- Barton Hills Elementary School Access, from the road that runs along the south side of the school

- Loop 360 Access, just east of MoPac, on the north side of Loop 360, where the trail is handicapped-accessible for a short distance

- Camp Craft Road Access, off Loop 360 in the Lost Creek Subdivision at the end of Scottish Woods Trail

- MoPac Access, from the southbound lane of MoPac just south of Loop 360. Instead of veering off onto the left entrance ramp to southbound MoPac, stay to the right to get to the greenbelt. Look for a sign to the greenbelt on the right.

In the past people commonly reached the greenbelt from the south side of Loop 360 across from and slightly to the north of Barton Creek Square Mall, but they crossed private property in doing so. The new MoPac Access makes it possible for people to reach the same stretch of the Barton Creek Greenbelt without trespassing on private land. Note, however, that the MoPac Access was not well designed for parking.

The most interesting but least accessible part of the trail lies between Loop 360 and Camp Craft Road. This section includes sheer cliff walls, lush vegetation, and a popular swimming area known as Twin Falls. Unfortunately, there is no off-street parking at the Camp Craft entrance; the best place to park is along Scottish Woods Trail. Portions of the trail may be impassable during high water unless you are prepared to wade across. The path along the greenbelt is narrower and rougher than the hike-and-bike trails described below.

Other popular greenbelts are the **Shoal Creek Greenbelt**, consisting of 57 acres in the downtown area, and the **Bull Creek Greenbelt**, which has 120 acres north of downtown and stretches northward from **Bull Creek District Park** to Loop 360. **Williamson Creek Greenbelt** has a half-mile trail west of IH 35 and south of Ben White Boulevard in the Battle Bend neighborhood. In East Austin, **Boggy Creek Greenbelt** passes through a nice pecan grove near Pleasant Valley Road and Rosewood Avenue. A **Trail of Trees** there helps you identify 35 species of trees along this trail. A brochure is available from PARD.

■ Hike-and-Bike Trails

PARD has developed an extensive trail system along creeks and streams in the Austin area. Most of the trails are 8-10 feet wide and well maintained with surfaces of finely crushed pink granite. Suitable for walking, jogging, or bicycling, the trails are so popular that they are often too crowded for normal cycling. The city is considering the construction of exclusive bicycle trails in certain areas to reduce pedestrian-cyclist congestion.

The **Town Lake Trail** extends along both sides of Town Lake from MoPac to Pleasant Valley Road (although the south side presently follows the sidewalk along Riverside Drive from Congress Avenue to Lakeshore Boulevard). The most popular section lies between Congress and MoPac, with a short connection from MoPac (Austin High School) to Deep Eddy Pool. Parking is available at Auditorium Shores, beneath the MoPac bridge at both Austin High School and Zilker Park, and behind the Parks and Recreation Department's building at Riverside and Lamar.

The **Shoal Creek Trail** connects with the Town Lake Trail east of Lamar Boulevard and extends northward to 38th Street, passing through Duncan Park and Pease Park. Although partially damaged by frequent flooding that has left it impassable at the lower end, the trail is mostly intact north of 15th Street. This is one of Austin's longest and most beautiful trails. Cliff walls and native woodlands between 26th and 32nd Streets are especially attractive.

The **Waller Creek Trail** diverges from the Town Lake Trail near the foot of Trinity Street and extends past the new Convention Center, through the hustle and bustle of 6th Street, past the outdoor theater at Symphony Square, and through Waterloo Park to the University of Texas campus at Martin Luther King, Jr., Boulevard.

The **Johnson Creek Trail** connects with the Town Lake Trail below the MoPac bridge over the Colorado River and extends nearly a mile to **Westenfield Park** at 2008 Enfield Road.

The **Blunn Creek Trail** begins at East Riverside and Alameda Drive and winds through Stacy Park in the Travis Heights area of South Austin, ending at the warm aquifer-fed Stacy Pool near Live

Oak Street. A **Trail of Trees** has been created along a portion of the trail. A guide to the 30 species along the way can be obtained from PARD. By following Alta Vista Drive from Live Oak to Oltorf Street, you can continue through the **Blunn Creek Nature Preserve**. (See Chapter 2, *At the Park,* for more information on this preserve.)

◼ Short Walks

Central Austin offers many opportunities for dayhikes through pleasant residential neighborhoods and historic areas. The Austin Convention and Visitor's Bureau and the Austin Historic Landmark Commission sponsor free walking tours of historic downtown Austin at 9 a.m. Thursday through Saturday and 2 p.m. Sundays. Tours begin at the south entrance to the Capitol and last approximately 2 hours. Call 478-0098 for information.

The **Capitol Grounds** at 11th and Congress are beautiful any season of the year. Austin citizens have used the area for recreation since 1849. The present capitol building celebrated its centennial in 1988 and recently underwent an extensive renovation.

Congress Avenue and **East 6th Street** are both designated historic districts that display many fine examples of nineteenth century commercial architecture. Free guided walking tours of these districts are offered, Thursday through Sunday, March through November, by the Austin Visitor's Center, 201 East 2nd St. (478-0098). The 2-hour tours leave from the south entrance of the Capitol, weather permitting.

From the Congress Avenue bridge over Town Lake, hundreds of thousands of Mexican Free-tailed Bats fly out early in the evening to search for insects and other food. Forming several ribbons or "columns" across the sky, these bats are a sight to behold. (See Chapter 6, *Out with Fauna and Friends,* for information on the best viewing area.)

Another area of architectural or historic interest is the **Bremond Block** at the southwest corner of 8th and Guadalupe Streets, a unique collection of nineteenth century residences in a variety of styles. While you're in this neighborhood, walk over to **Treaty Oak**

Park, a block west of Lamar Boulevard between 5th and 6th Streets. Estimated to be 500-600 years old, the live oak tree known as Treaty Oak was poisoned in 1989, catching the attention of the world. While it has lost its majesty, the tree clings to life, and people still come to pay homage to it.

Brush Square is another good place downtown, at 401 East 5th Street, where a big old tree is perfect for storytelling outdoors. Next to it is **O'Henry Museum**, which was once the home of William Sydney Porter (O'Henry). This museum is now listed on the National Register of Historic Sites.

Numerous structures can be found along Nueces Street, Rio Grande Street, and West Avenue between 6th Street and Martin Luther King, Jr., Boulevard. The **Hyde Park** neighborhood, bounded by 38th, Guadalupe, 45th, and Duval Streets, was developed in the 1880s as one of Austin's first suburbs. Still predominantly residential, it contains several notable buildings constructed by early settlers. Tours of some of the homes are offered every spring by the Hyde Park Neighborhood Association.

Other distinctive residential areas for pleasant day hikes include **West Austin, Enfield,** and **Brykerwoods** (located generally between Lamar and MoPac between 5th and 35th Streets). In south Austin, the most notable areas are **Travis Heights** and **Fairview Park**, bounded roughly by Riverside Drive, Kenwood Avenue, Live Oak Street, and Newning Avenue.

A stroll through **Waterloo Park** is a short but lovely walk, with plenty of places to sit and ponder. Waller Creek runs through this downtown park at 403 East 15th Street, lending it added beauty. Because the park is relatively large considering its central location, it is a choice spot for many special events.

The **University of Texas** offers nicely landscaped grounds, several fountains, and buildings in a variety of styles. Weatherproof maps at several locations help with orientation. Be sure to make it over to **the Drag**, the strip of Guadalupe Street that adjoins the campus. At 23rd and Guadalupe, street vendors display handmade jewelry, photographs, clothing, and many other items in the outdoor market.

Laguna Gloria, at the west end of 35th Street on Lake Austin, is a Spanish colonial-style estate that houses an art museum. A beautiful oak-canopied trail follows the edge of the lagoon to the end of the property. The big event of the year at Laguna Gloria is Fiesta, an art fair held the third weekend of May that attracts artists from all over the country.

Nearby **Mt. Bonnell** towers above Lake Austin and offers wonderful views of the Austin skyline and Westlake Hills. Turn right off West 35th onto Mount Bonnell Road and follow it to the parking area at the base of the mountain. Take the steps to the top, or walk to the north end and climb a less demanding trail.

▌Music Outdoors

Austin has a variety of outdoor musical venues, most of which are inexpensive if not free. Across from Barton Springs Pool on summer weekend nights, people spread a blanket out to enjoy musicals, concerts, ballet, and other performances at **Zilker Hillside Theater**. Not far away, **Auditorium Shores**, at Riverside Drive and South First Street, is a popular site for concerts, especially on July 4th and during Aqua Festival, one of the city's biggest events held annually in August. A particularly unique showplace is **Symphony Square**, at 11th and Red River Streets, where a small moat separates the performers' stage from the audience, and a high bridge at one end connects the two. The music there varies from blues and jazz to brass quintets, string quartets, and guitar. Performances run from May through August on Friday and Saturday nights and sometimes on Sunday, too. Wednesdays are devoted to activities for children (see Chapter 8, *For Special People,* for more information). For program information call 476-6064.

Other locations for outdoor music include **Wooldridge Square** downtown at 9th and Guadalupe Streets, the **State Capitol** grounds, **East 6th Street**, and **Stacy Park** south of the river and east of Congress Avenue. Somewhat farther out, **Northwest Park**, at Ardath and Elise Streets, hosts free outdoor concerts, too. Call PARD, Cultural Arts Division, at 477-5824 for details or check the "XL ent." section of the *Austin American-Statesman,* published each Thursday. Another good source of information is the University of Texas at 471-2787 or P.O. Box 7818, Austin, Texas, 78712. Ask to be placed on the mailing list for the UT Fine Arts Calendar. No calendar, however, can anticipate the impromptu sessions that spring up on "the Drag," that stretch of Guadalupe Street around 24th Street on the UT campus. Impromptu sessions are also common on 6th Street and other locations in this music-oriented city. Austin offers music for everyone.

■ Moonlight Towers

Unique in all the world, Austin's moonlight towers are the only remaining examples of the tower lighting system popular in U.S. cities during the nineteenth century. During the period 1894-1895, 31 towers were erected at various locations throughout Austin. The towers are 150 feet high, built of cast and wrought iron, and mounted on a 15-foot iron pedestal anchored in concrete. Each tower illuminates a circle 3,000 feet in diameter. Only 17 of the original towers still stand.

The moonlight towers were designated as State Archaeological Landmarks in 1970 and listed in the National Register of Historic Places in 1975. In 1985, following a unanimous recommendation by the City Council, Austin voters approved a revenue bond package for the restoration of the 17 original towers, to be completed in time for the 100th "birthday" of the moonlight towers.

A replica tower in Zilker Park (on Town Lake) serves as a giant Christmas tree when a cone of colored lights is attached to the tower every December. Since 1967 this 150-foot "tree," visible from many vantage points throughout the city, has been the focal point for Austin's Yule Fest Celebration. The Christmas tree lighting ceremony traditionally occurs on the first Sunday in December, followed by the opening of Santa's Village. Throughout the Yule Fest Celebration, crowds flock to the Trail of Lights, a circle of fabulous lighted displays through Zilker Park, and the Christmas lights that decorate the trees at the nearby Austin Area Garden Center. A favorite pastime at night is to visit the neighborhoods and individual houses whose Christmas decorations are so exceptionally beautiful that they are publicized in the newspapers in and around Austin.

PUBLICATIONS

Martyn-Baker, Julie, Ron Fieseler, and Butch Smith, eds. *Hill Country Oasis*. Austin, Texas: Austin Parks and Recreation Department, Barton Springs/Edwards Aquifer Conservation District, and Save Barton Creek Association, 1992.

McLeod, Gerald and Tom Grisham. *Barton Creek Guide*. Austin, Texas: *Austin Chronicle*, 1992.

National Off-Road Bicycle. *Trail Map, Barton Creek Greenbelt: Loop 360 to Zilker*. Manchaca, Texas: Breakthrough Publications, 1988.

Pipkin, Turk, and Marshall Frech, eds. *Barton Springs Eternal: The Soul of a City*. Austin, Texas: Softshoe Publishing, Hill Country Foundation, 1993.

AT
THE
PARK 2

■ City Parks

Austin parks come in many sizes and serve a variety of functions. The major categories, from small to large, are neighborhood parks (including school parks), district parks, and metropolitan parks. Greenbelts, described in Chapter 1, are a special category. Generally long and narrow, they follow creeks, rivers, or scenic ravines. Preserves, another category, are lands set aside for the purpose of protecting flora and fauna native to the area. Little maintenance is provided to greenbelts and preserves.

Unbeknownst to some, the city designates certain places throughout its park system as reservation areas, which you may reserve for your family or group of friends (see Appendix 2, *Agencies*). For example, you may reserve **Eilers Park**, mentioned in Chapter 1, which is centrally located next to Deep Eddy Pool. Such parks are popular, however, so make reservations well in advance.

Some 200 parks, recreation centers, and other outdoor facilities are managed by the City of Austin, far too many to name them all here. Those that are described below were selected for their size, broad appeal, or distinctive features. Together they convey the variety of resources that Austin has to offer.

METROPOLITAN PARKS

Metropolitan parks are large and best equipped to suit a variety of people, whatever their interests.

- **Emma Long Metropolitan Park/City Park**, in west Austin on the north bank of Lake Austin (346-1831)

- **Commons Ford Metropolitan Park**, on the south shore of Lake Austin (263-5478)

- **Circle C Metropolitan Park**, in southwest Austin

- **Lake Walter E. Long Metropolitan Park**, in east Austin (926-5230)

- **Mary Moore Searight Metropolitan Park**, in south Austin

- **Slaughter Creek Metropolitan Park**, in southwest Austin

- **Town Lake Metropolitan Park**, in central Austin (480-8318)

- **Walnut Creek Metropolitan Park**, in north Austin (834-0824)

- **Zilker Metropolitan Park**, in south Austin (476-6922)

Commons Ford Metropolitan Park, on the south shore of Lake Austin, and **Circle C Metropolitan Park**, in southwest Austin, at Slaughter Lane and MoPac, are recent acquisitions in the category of metropolitan parks. Commons Ford, 614 Commons Ford Road, has lake access and facilities for rental.

Emma Long Metropolitan Park, best known as **City Park**, teems with people out to enjoy swimming or boating on the north bank of Lake Austin. Boat ramps and docks are designed for both motor and sailboats, while swimmers have a wading pool and a bathhouse to use. An open playing field, volleyball, and archery range appeal to the sports enthusiasts, while others can enjoy the scenic picnic areas with barbecue pits and reservation areas. Situated along beautiful Lake Austin, City Park can be reached by taking RM 2222 west past

Loop 360. Half a mile after passing Loop 360, turn left onto City Park Road. After 6.5 miles the road ends at the park. Expect an entry fee.

Lake Walter E. Long Metropolitan Park, on the far east side of town, is immense. Spread out over 7,656 acres, it is the city's largest park. With 2 large boat ramps and wide-open banks, activities vary from canoeing and sailing to volleyball and picnics. Certain areas may be reserved for group gatherings. To reach the park take Decker Lane, turn east on Decker Lake Road and go 1.5 miles.

A relatively new park in far south Austin is **Mary Moore Searight Metropolitan Park** at 907 Slaughter Lane. It butts up against Slaughter Creek, and Little Slaughter Creek meanders around the main facilities, which include a picnic pavilion, disc golf course, and courts for baseball, basketball, soccer, tennis, and volleyball. The trail system features a hike-and-bike trail, an equestrian trail, and a paved trail for people with disabilities. Native Indiangrass and rare Texas bluebell flowers grow here. An alternate access point is in the Texas Oaks subdivision at the end of Decker Prairie Drive.

Slaughter Creek Metropolitan Park is a relatively new city park in the southwest area that has 412 acres, making it larger than Zilker, which has 351 acres. The main attraction is a veloway, a 3.1-mile track for bicycles and rollerblading (see *Bicycling* in Chapter 3). Besides the veloway, the park includes picnic tables, a playground, basketball and volleyball courts, soccer fields, and a disc golf course. To reach the main entrance to the veloway, take MoPac south of Slaughter Lane and turn left onto LaCrosse Avenue, which takes you to the entrance.

Walnut Creek Metropolitan Park, along North Lamar Boulevard south of Coxville Road, includes a maze of trails along 3 branches of Walnut Creek. Other trail segments also exist farther downstream on Walnut Creek, but they have not yet been integrated into a complete system. The most accessible trail adjoins **Jourdan-Bachman Pioneer Farm** (837-1215), which is a replica of a nineteenth-century farm settlement located at 11418 Sprinkle Cutoff Road.

Both **Town Lake** and **Zilker Metropolitan Parks** are described in Chapter 1. They are the heart and soul of outdoors Austin, but others attract nearly as many people, especially on weekends.

DISTRICT PARKS

While not as large and multifunctional as metropolitan parks, district parks are still quite large.

Bull Creek District Park is accessible from Loop 360 south of Spicewood Springs Road or at the intersection of Loop 360 and Lakewood Drive. The trail there is a pleasant retreat in spite of the proximity of Loop 360 traffic. Nearby is **Upper Bull Creek District Park**, on the south side of Spicewood Springs Road 2 miles west of Loop 360.

A park that opened in April, 1994, is **Dick Nichols District Park** in southwest Austin. Named for a member of the City Council during the late 1960s and early 1970s, Dick Nichols Park has 150 acres with Williamson Creek running through it. Park plans include a swimming pool and trail access from Convict Hill Road where it intersects Brush Country Road/Latta Drive. Take William Cannon Drive west past MoPac and turn left (south) onto Beckett Road, which will take you to the park entrance. The address is 8011 Beckett Road.

Of all the district parks, the most notable is **Pease Park**, which runs along Shoal Creek as it flows north-south. In fact Pease Park is only one of a string of parks and greenbelts that runs along Shoal Creek as it flows all the way into Town Lake. It's easy to fuse in your mind what the City of Austin calls **Seider Springs Park**, **Pease Park**, **Duncan Park**, and the **Shoal Creek Greenbelt** (see *Greenbelts* in Chapter 1). Besides being centrally located, these areas are truly beautiful even when the creek bed is dry in places. A wading pool makes Pease Park particularly nice for the little folks, and people of all ages enjoy the wild and crazy spring bash known as Eeyore's Birthday Party. Pease Park hugs the west side of Lamar Boulevard, so it's easy to find, especially between Enfield Road and Windsor Road.

Other district parks are scattered throughout the city:

■ **Balcones District Park**, in northwest Austin, 12017 Amherst Drive

■ **Bartholomew District Park**, in east Austin, 1800 East 51st Street (928-0014)

- **Garrison District Park**, in southwest Austin at 6001 Manchaca Road (441-2772)

- **Givens District Park and Recreation Center**, in east Austin at 3811 East 12th Street (928-1982)

- **Mabel Davis District Park**, in south Austin at 3427 Parker Lane (441-5247)

- **Northeast District Park**, east of U.S. Highway 183 and thus outside the central loop of Austin, at 5909 Coolbrook Drive

- **Northwest District Park and Recreation Center**, in north Austin at 7000 Ardath Street (458-4107)

- **Onion Creek District Park**, in south Austin near Pleasant Valley Road and Onion Creek Drive

SMALLER PARKS

Just as Shoal Creek runs through a string of places that seem to blend together, Boggy Creek does likewise in east Austin. From north to south, respectively, you have **Downs/Mabson Field**, **Rosewood Park and Recreation Center**, **Parque Zaragoza Park and Recreation Center** (472-7142), and the **Boggy Creek Greenbelt** (see *Greenbelts* in Chapter 1).

Dittmar Park and Recreation Center (441-4777) is a relatively new site in south Austin between Manchaca Road and South 1st Street at 1009 West Dittmar Road. This park has many recreational facilities available.

Dottie Jordan Park and Recreation Center (926-3491), in northeast Austin at 2803 Loyola Lane, is particularly nice, situated as it is along Walnut Creek. Recreational programs are designed for a wide variety of ages, all the way from kindergartners to senior citizens.

Mayfield Park and Preserve, on West 35th Street next to Laguna Gloria was donated in 1971 by Mary Mayfield Gutsch. The park surrounds a house and 5 lily ponds, while the preserve consists of 23 acres of woodlands, meadows, and waterways. Trails there cross Barrow Brook and Taylor Branch Creeks. This park, known especially for its peacocks, is appreciated for its beauty and serenity by children and adults alike.

In south central Austin at **Stacy Park**—or more precisely Big and Little Stacy Park—one can stroll a pleasantly shaded hike-and-bike trail that follows Blunn Creek. One of the park's special features is a warm-water swimming pool that stays open year-round.

■ Preserves

The Austin area presently boasts 12 nature preserves, which are sanctuaries containing significant natural communities, species, or unique natural features. These preserves are intended for activities which are gentle on the habitat, such as birdwatching, nature walks, and photography. The preserves are carefully managed to minimize disturbance to erodible areas and wildlife habitats. When visiting a preserve you should stay on the marked paths and leave all plants and animals undisturbed. Please leave your own pets at home. Pack out what you pack in. Take only pictures—leave only footprints.

The City of Austin manages several preserves. For more information on each one, contact the Nature Preserves Office at 327-5437.

Barrow Preserve is a 10-acre area in the Bull Creek watershed that includes a small perennial spring. The trailhead is off Long Point Drive on Step Down Cove. It is especially nice to visit in April when the wild red and yellow columbines are blooming.

Bee Creek Preserve, on Redbud Trail just west of Tom Miller Dam, is a 66-acre preserve with several trails originally established by the Travis Audubon Society.

Blunn Creek Nature Preserve lies north of St. Edwards Drive, half a mile west of IH 35. Several trails traverse the preserve, including a paved wheelchair-accessible trail, which can be reached from the west side of Travis High School. This trail was built in 1991 as a project of REI, with assistance from members of the Austin Sierra Club.

Forest Ridge Preserve has a shady, picturesque trail that runs 1 mile along the southern cliffs of the 414-acre preserve and over-looks Bull Creek. Park your car at a gravel lot by the creek on the west side of Loop 360 0.6 miles south of Spicewood Springs Road. The trail also features a dry-foot stepping stone crossing of the creek. The preserve is Golden-cheeked Warbler habitat.

Indiangrass Preserve on Lake Walter E. Long protects 200 acres of the vanishing Blackland Prairie. Once covering 12 million acres in Texas and extending north into Canada, the Blackland Prairie was an ocean of grassland that early settlers discovered for agriculture; today, less than 1 percent of the original prairie remains undisturbed. In addition to such native grass species as big and little bluestem, sideoats grama, tall grama, and the Indiangrass for which it is named, the Austin preserve contains such lovely wildflowers as gayfeather and Texas bluebells. It also affords wonderful opportunities to see migratory birds. One must arrange a visit with the Nature Preserves Office ahead of time, but to reach the preserve, take U.S. Highway 290 east to FM 3177, turn right and go half a mile to Lindell, turn left and go 1 mile to Blue Bluff.

Mayfield Preserve, see Mayfield Park and Preserve under Smaller Parks in this chapter.

Onion Creek Preserve is a 180-acre sanctuary located along Texas Highway 71 East. Purchased for its excellent wildlife habitat, it contains several groves of pecan trees and the rare native Texas bluegrass. Because the area must be reached through an easement across private property, it can be visited only by prior arrangement with the Nature Preserves Office.

Vireo Preserve, acquired to help protect nesting sites of the endangered Black-capped Vireo songbird, is adjacent to Wild Basin on Loop 360. Due to the sensitivity of the habitat, visitation is by prior arrangement with the Nature Preserves Office only.

In the early 1970s, 7 women saw a pristine area of the Hill Country in danger of being developed. Thus began an amazing success story: the creation of a wilderness park with no major donor and little political support. Small donations and a variety of fund-raisers provided the bulk of funds used to obtain a matching Land and Water Conservation Fund grant in the late 1970s.

The resulting **Wild Basin Wilderness Preserve** (327-7622) has 2.5 miles of trails and encompasses 227 acres of eastern Hill Country, which has steeper slopes and thinner soils than the Hill Country farther west. Bee Creek courses through the basin, dropping at one point over 15-foot waterfalls. Brown's Hollow and North Hollow join the creek at the heart of the basin, creating a level park like area with deeper soils at the center of the preserve. Thus several microenvironments exist close together, which support a wider variety of life-forms than one usually finds in such a small area. The endangered Golden-cheeked Warbler and Black-capped Vireo are known to nest in Wild Basin and nearby terrain.

The interpretive program includes guided tours for children, school groups, families, and the general public. Walks in the preserve focus on plant life, birds, snakes, other animals and their habitat, and geology. Stargazing and full-moon walks are also offered occasionally.

Perhaps the most notable feature is the easy-access trail. A service project of REI, this loop trail on the upper ridge was leveled to accommodate wheelchairs and other mobility limitations. Following a severe rain, however, it is best to call to inquire about the latest trail conditions.

While Travis County holds the title to the property, Wild Basin Wilderness, a nonprofit organization, manages the resources and interpretive activities. The county provides 20 percent of the funding. For the remainder, Wild Basin depends on public support and always welcomes donations, volunteers, and memberships. The grounds are open daily from dawn to dusk, while the education building is open 9 a.m. to 4:30 p.m. Monday through Friday and 9 a.m. to 5 p.m. Saturday and Sunday. Wild Basin is located on the east side of Loop 360, 1.5 miles north of Bee Caves Road. No pets are allowed, on or off leash.

Hamilton Pool Preserve (264-2740) centers on a pool and grotto formed when the dome of a cave collapsed thousands of years ago. A 65-foot waterfall, lush plant communities, and huge bald cypress trees are some of the attractions of this special site. A one-mile trail follows Hamilton Creek from the pool to the Pedernales River. Take Texas Highway 71 west to RM 3238 (Hamilton Pool Road) and continue 13 miles to the park entrance near the Pedernales River crossing. Expect a fee.

Westcave Preserve (210/825-3442) is a 30-acre nature sanctuary owned and operated by the private nonprofit Westcave Preserve Corporation, located less than a mile past Hamilton Pool. One of the most beautiful spots in Travis County, it is a collapsed grotto thick with ferns. Because the area is environmentally sensitive, pets are not permitted and visitation is by guided tours only, which are scheduled at 10 a.m., 12 noon, 2 p.m., and 4 p.m. on weekends. Lasting an hour and 15 minutes, the tours are limited to the first 30 people to sign up, yet reservations are not accepted. Donations are requested. Take Texas Highway 71 west through Bee Caves, turn onto RM 3238, and drive 14 miles to the preserve, which will be on the right just after you climb out of the Pedernales River gorge.

Zilker Nature Preserve (327-5437) features an ephemeral creek edged with meadow, streamside habitats, and a high cliff with shallow caves. A rock-walled ramada overlooks the preserve and downtown Austin. Wooley croton bush and myrtle croton as well as mountain laurel are in abundance.

County Parks

The Travis County park system provides a variety of activities at each of its 26 locations. From the rugged cliffs and lakes of **Pace Bend Recreation Area** in the Hill Country to the quiet, lush lands of **Webberville Park**, Travis County offers something for every outdoor enthusiast. A fee is charged at many of the parks. For information and reservations, call the county at 473-9437 between 8 a.m. and 5 p.m., Monday through Friday. You may get a recording plus room for a message, and return calls can sometimes be slow.

In the basic descriptions below, restrooms are available unless specified otherwise, but overnight use and camping are not permitted unless mentioned specifically.

In northwest Travis County, many of the parks are owned by the Lower Colorado River Authority but managed by the county.

Allen Park, near MoPac and Hart Lane on Westside Drive, has 10 acres with group shelters and hiking and nature trails.

Fritz Hughes Park, with only 5 acres, has a boat launch on the banks of Lake Austin just below Mansfield Dam, off Low Water Crossing Road and Fritz Hughes Park Road.

Mary Quinlan Park along Lake Austin has 6 acres. This park offers a swimming area and a boat launch. From RM 620 turn onto Quinlan Park Road and go 5.5 miles to the end of the road.

Selma Hughes Park also offers a swimming area and a boat launch. Also small with just 5 acres, this park, too, lies along Lake Austin. Take RM 2222 west, turn left onto RM 620 and go about 2 miles, then turn left (south) onto Quinlan Park Road; after 4 to 5 miles, turn left onto Selma Hughes Park Road, and drive another mile or so to reach the park at the end of the road.

Two often forgotten areas are **Webberville Park** and **Richard Moya Park**, both situated in east Travis County. Webberville Park, on the banks of the Colorado River, combines flat terrain with rolling hills. The thickly wooded park has nature trails that wind deep into the heart of its 135 acres. This park, which also offers group shelters, a boat launch, and athletic fields, is located on FM 969 3 miles east of the town of Webberville. **Little Webberville Park** is a much smaller 6-acre area in Webberville itself that offers a boat launch. Starting from the intersection of U.S. Highway 183 and FM 969, go 15 miles east on FM 969 and turn right on Water Street, which runs into the park.

Richard Moya Park, along the banks of Onion Creek, is thick with trees and interesting scenery. Its athletic fields and nature trails, spread over 105 acres, are 2 of the main attractions. Group shelters are also available. This nice park is approximately 3 miles east of U.S. Highway 183 on Burleson Road, along Onion Creek.

Manor Park is a small area, with just 5 acres, located off Carrie Manor Road at the East Rural Community Center in Manor.

Among the popular spots in southwest Travis County is **Loop 360 Park**, situated on the south shore of Lake Austin directly under the Loop 360 bridge. This small area of just 5 acres is good for swimming and launching boats into Lake Austin amidst a beautiful view of the area.

Windmill Run has good nature trails for hiking. This area of 50 acres can be reached from the Y intersection at Oak Hill by going west on Texas Highway 71. Turn left on Scenic Brook Drive and then left on Kirkham Cove. The park is at the end of the cove.

A bit farther from Austin, a 10-mile trail encircles **Lake Georgetown**, winding through the cedar brakes and passing a nice waterfall near a former truck farm along the north shoreline. To reach the trail, travel north on IH 35 to Georgetown, take the RM 2338 exit, turn left, and go about 3 miles to the park entry. Turn left on the entry road, drive across the dam, and follow the signs to the trail head on the south shore of the lake. This trail is maintained by the Corps of Engineers (255-8567).

■ LCRA Parks

The Lower Colorado River Authority (LCRA) has many dedicated parks, with almost 3,400 acres of land throughout its district, which stretches along the Colorado River all the way from San Saba County to the Gulf Coast. The agency owns and manages an additional 16,000 acres of land, much of which the public uses for recreation. LCRA's parks information department, 3701 Lake Austin Boulevard, (473-4083 or 800/776-5272 ext. 4083) distributes brochures describing each lake, park, program, and primitive recreation site under its jurisdiction. Be sure to ask for the succinct fact sheet "Sources of Park Information," which provides phone numbers for parks managed by LCRA, Travis County, City of Austin Parks and Recreation Department, the state, and federal entities. The fact sheet also lists resources for area maps, the most popular parks, pertinent Chambers of Commerce, boat rental spots by each lake or bay, lodging near each lake, Lake Travis marinas, Austin swimming pools, and LCRA's dam statistics.

Fifteen miles northwest of Austin, Mansfield Dam divides Lake Austin to the south from Lake Travis to the north. LCRA has 12 parks along Lake Austin and Lake Travis, while other parks lie outside the area covered by this book. The three parks along Lake Austin—Fritz Hughes, Mary Quinlan, and Selma Hughes—were described in the previous section (see *County Parks*). Nine Lake Travis parks, owned by LCRA but operated by Travis County, are **Arkansas Bend, Cypress Creek, Dink Pearson, Mansfield Dam Recreation Area, McGregor Park** (also called **Hippie Hollow**), **Pace Bend Recreation Area, Sandy Creek, Tom**

Hughes, and **Bob Wentz Park at Windy Point** (another park, **Camp Creek**, is operated by Burnet County). All LCRA/Travis County parks charge an admission fee, the amount of which depends upon the park, number of people, and whether you are camping or launching a boat. Travis County offers annual entrance permits for frequent visitors. Contact the county (473-9437) to determine the actual cost of any planned events. In general, campsites may be used up to a limit of 7 days.

Arkansas Bend Park is a large park with 663 acres, 12 campsites, a boat ramp, hiking trails, and a restroom but no potable water. Take U.S. Highway 183 north, turn left onto RM 1431, continue to Lohmans Crossing where you turn left again; turn left again onto Sylvester Ford Road and go 3 miles down this road to reach Arkansas Bend.

Cypress Creek has 37 acres, with 10 campsites, a boat ramp, and a restroom but no potable water. From RM 620, turn west onto RM 2769. The park is located at the intersection of RM 2769 and Old Anderson Mill Road.

Dink Pearson Park, with just 4 acres, offers swimming, primitive camping, and a boat launch. It is located along Lake Travis at the end of Lohmans Crossing Road in Point Venture.

Mansfield Dam Recreation Area, with 71 acres, offers 36 campsites, a boat ramp, and a restroom. Here potable water is available. From the intersection of U.S. Highway 183 and RM 620, go approximately 13.5 miles west on RM 620. An alternate route is to take RM 2222 west for 11 miles to RM 620 and turn south onto RM 620, which curves to the west for another 6 miles. The entrance

to the park is on the west side of the dam.

McGregor Park/Hippie Hollow is somewhat larger with
109 acres. There are hiking trails but no camping, and swimming is
allowed in designated places, but there is no boat ramp. The
restroom is equipped for people with disabilities. No potable water
is provided. Take RM 2222 west to RM 620, turn south onto
RM 620, and then turn right on Comanche Trail, following Comanche Trail for about 1.6 miles. After you pass Oasis Bluff Drive
on the right, look for the park on your left.

Pace Bend Recreation Area (264-1482) is immense. Spread out
over 1,520 acres, it has 420 campsites, 20 recreational vehicle sites,
shower facilities, and potable water. Pace Bend Park stretches
across a peninsula 4 miles long bordered by Lake Travis. You have
a choice between gently sloping beach on the eastern side for
swimming and boating or high cliffs and coves on the western side.
No less than 22 coves have been named. The center of the peninsula
serves as a natural wildlife preserve to deer, raccoons, opossum,
rabbits, and many bird species. No vehicles are permitted in the
interior. From the Y intersection of U.S. Highway 290 and Texas
Highway 71, take Texas Highway 71 about 13 miles to RM 2322,
turn right onto RM 2322, and go about 4.6 miles.

Sandy Creek is small, a mere 25 acres, yet it offers 31 campsites, a
boat ramp, hiking trails, potable water, and a restroom equipped for
people with disabilities. From the intersection of U.S. Highway 183
and RM 1431, go west on RM 1431 for 1.8 miles, turn left onto Lime
Creek Road, and then go about 6 miles to the intersection of Sandy
Creek Arm and Lime Creek.

Tom Hughes Park, with 5 acres, charges an entrance fee for
swimming. This park sits along Lake Travis at the end of Park
Drive approximately half a mile off RM 620.

Bob Wentz Park at Windy Point (266-3857) is also small with
just 23 acres. Deserving of its name, it attracts sailors and
windsurfers as well as swimmers and scuba divers. Camping is
primitive, and there is no boat ramp or potable water. Take
RM 2222 west to RM 620, turn left (south) onto RM 620, turn right
onto Comanche Trail, and follow Comanche Trail about 3 miles,
passing McGregor Park (Hippie Hollow) on the way. The park is off
Comanche Trail a bit farther down.

Camp Creek Park is a large park of 600 acres of pecan bottoms on the upper reaches of Lake Travis. Operated by Burnet County, the park has a boat ramp and picnic tables but no potable water and no restrooms. Take RM 1431 from Marble Falls to County Road 343. The park entrance is half a mile away.

LCRA has a Primitive Recreation System. The 6 primitive areas are along the northwest Highland Lakes, mostly between Pace Bend Park and Lake Marble Falls. The primitive areas, which are meant to be enjoyed in their natural state, are suitable for camping, picnicking, hiking, nature study, photography, and birdwatching.

An innovative program developed by LCRA is the Colorado River Trail program, designed to develop tourism and recreational facilities along LCRA's 500-mile Colorado River corridor, which stretches from San Saba county to Matagorda county where the river empties into Matagorda Bay. The trail consists of the Colorado River, its lakes, public highways, railroad rights-of-way, parks, and scenic areas. Contact the LCRA in Austin at 473-4083 or 800/776-5272 ext. 4083 for more information. Be sure to request the Explorer's Map published to promote the Trail program. This colorfully illustrated map highlights the cultural, recreational, historical, agricultural, and environmental attractions found in LCRA's district.

LCRA has regulations for the lands and waters under its jurisdiction. It is against state law to hunt with, possess, or shoot a firearm, bow, crossbow, slingshot, or any weapon on or across the lands of the LCRA.

■ State Parks

Austin area residents are fortunate in having a number of state parks nearby. In less than 3 hours, Enchanted Rock is at hand, and well within an hour McKinney Falls can be reached. Other popular spots are Inks Lake, Pedernales Falls, and Bastrop and Buescher State Parks. For reservations at all state parks call 389-9900.

Pine trees are uncommon in the Central Texas area, except for a thriving stand east of Austin in the area between Bastrop and Smithville, about an hour's drive away. The lost pines are found in 2 state parks, **Bastrop** and **Buescher**, which are connected by

Park Road 1. Hiking, swimming, and camping are available.

Bastrop State Park (512/321-2101) is located 30 miles east of
Austin in the Lost Pines region, an area isolated from the main
body of East Texas pine forests by nearly 100 miles. The park has
3,503 acres and offers an 8.5-mile hiking trail constructed through
the efforts of the Texas Trails Association and the Sierra Club. It is
especially nice in winter when the yaupon hollies are thick with
berries, and in spring when the occasional dogwoods are in bloom.
Campsites range from primitive camping to cabins, and activities
include hiking, backpacking, and swimming. Showers and hookups
are available. Take Texas Highway 71 east to Bastrop; turn left on
Texas Highway 95 and right on Texas Highway 21 to Park Road 1.

Personnel at Bastrop State Park can provide information on Lake
Bastrop, an area of 785 acres with limited use by permit only.

Buescher State Park (512/237-2241) shares many of the characteristics of Bastrop but is generally less crowded. It is farther east
and much smaller, with 1,016 acres. A 7.7-mile hiking trail winds
through the park. Camping, hiking, and swimming are common,
and restrooms, showers, and hookups are available. Follow the
directions to Bastrop State Park and continue along Park Road 1 for
13 miles to Buescher State Park. Or take Texas Highway 71 east to
Smithville and turn left on FM 153 for half a mile.

Colorado Bend State Park (915/628-3240) has a 2-mile hiking
trail along Gorman Creek. This is a primitive park with few conve-
niences. Take U.S. Highway 183 to Lampasas, turn left on FM 580,
and continue to the town of Bend. Follow directional signs along
6 miles of unpaved roads to the park. Gorman Falls and Cave, one
of the park's most alluring features, is open only to guided tours, as
are several other caves.

One of the more unique sites nearby is **Enchanted Rock State
Natural Area** (915/247-3903), with 1,643 acres. Located between
Fredericksburg and Llano, it takes less than 3 hours to reach. The
granite dome is one of the largest of its kind in the United States,
second only to Stone Mountain in Georgia. A climb to the summit is
an exhilarating experience that offers spectacular views of the
surrounding countryside. A 4-mile loop trail encircles the massive
rock formations. Other trails pass between and over the formations,
and you can even crawl through a cave that passes through them.

Besides hiking, Enchanted Rock affords excellent rock climbing and backpacking. There are walk-in campsites but no vehicular camping. Facilities include a playground, picnic areas, showers, and restrooms. Take U.S. Highway 290 west to Fredericksburg; turn right on RM 965 and continue 18 miles to the park.

Guadalupe River State Park (210/438-2656), as the name indicates, is located on the Guadalupe River. With 1,938 acres, this is a large park with good picnic facilities, campsites, a playground, a day-use group facility, swimming, restrooms, and showers. Go south on IH 35 to New Braunfels, then west on Texas Highway 46 for 29 miles. The park office also provides information on a 2-mile, 2-hour tour of the adjoining **Honey Creek State Natural Area,** which is conducted at 9 a.m. every Saturday. No fee is charged for this tour, but voluntary donations are suggested. Honey Creek has nature trails for hiking.

Inks Lake State Park (512/793-2223), 1.5 hours northwest of Austin, is one of several state parks amid the Highland Lakes. Seven miles of hiking trails wind through the granite hillsides above Inks Lake. Swimming, canoeing, water skiing, and even pedal boat rentals are offered, while other activities include picnics, hiking trails, and backpacking. With 1,200 acres, Inks Lake is especially beautiful in the spring when the bluebonnets are in bloom. Campsites range from primitive camping to screened shelters and group facilities, and showers are available. Take U.S. Highway 183 north to Seward Junction, then go left on Texas Highway 29. Nine miles past Burnet, turn left on Park Road 4.

Lyndon B. Johnson State Historical Park (210/644-2252) is in Stonewall, 15 miles west of Johnson City on U.S. Highway 290. Amenities include a group facility, hiking and nature trails, playground, picnic areas, and a swimming pool. The park also features the **Sauer-Beckmann Living History Farm**, which depicts turn-of-the-century German-Texan Hill Country life. Admission is free.

The state park visitor center is the departure point for National Park Service bus tours of the **Lyndon B. Johnson National Historical Park (LBJ Ranch Unit)** across the Pedernales River. These tours are conducted daily, except Christmas Day, from 10 a.m. to 4 p.m. and include the former president's birthplace, the Johnson family cemetery, and an exterior view of the Texas White House on the LBJ Ranch, where Lady Bird Johnson still resides.

The second unit of the **Lyndon B. Johnson National Historical Park** (210/868-7128) is in Johnson City, 1 block south of U.S. Highway 290 on 9th Street. Tours of the **LBJ Boyhood Home** are conducted daily, except Christmas and New Year's Day, every half hour from 9 a.m. to 5 p.m. Self-guided tours are available at the nearby Johnson Settlement.

Kerrville-Schreiner State Park (210/257-5392) has 7 miles of hiking trails through Hill Country terrain. It's a great place to camp during the grand Kerrville Folk Festival, held every year around Memorial Day and Labor Day. Take U.S. Highway 290 west to Fredericksburg, turn left on Texas Highway 16 to Kerrville, and 1 mile past town turn left on Texas Highway 173.

Lake Somerville Park contains 2 first-class parks located northwest of Brenham: the **Birch Creek** unit on the north side of the lake and the **Nails Creek** unit on the south side. Connecting them is the 21.6-mile Somerville Trailway, a unique backcountry trail that passes through dense stands of trees, past scenic overlooks, and over water crossings. The trail is suitable for hiking, biking, or equestrian use. The Birch Creek unit (409/535-7763) is 12 miles off Texas Highway 36 on Park Road 57, while the Nails Creek unit (409/289-2392) is located on FM 180, 15 miles off U.S. Highway 290.

Lockhart State Park (512/398-3479) features a playground, picnic area, swimming pool, and group facilities over a relatively small area of 263 acres. Address: Route 3, Box 69, Lockhart, Texas, 78644.

Longhorn Cavern State Park (512/756-4680) gives daily tours of Longhorn Cavern and the museum there. Picnics are also possible in this 639-acre park.

McKinney Falls State Park (243-1643), at the confluence of Onion Creek and Williamson Creek, draws many from the Austin area because of its proximity. Depending on the part of town from which you are traveling, the trip to this 640-acre park 13 miles southeast of the State Capitol can take as little as 15 minutes or as long as 45. Hiking ranges from an easy 3.25-mile hike-and-bike trail that loops through the park to a more rugged half-mile interpretive trail deep in the woods through the cliffs above Onion Creek. Camping and surface bicycling are permitted, and a playground, restrooms, and showers are available.

Favorite spots are the upper falls of Onion Creek behind the Smith Visitor Center and McKinney Falls farther downstream. In 1981 the park was closed to swimming because of pollution primarily from a sewage treatment plant that was later closed. Thanks to the hard work of park officials and volunteers, swimming was resumed in 1993. It's a good idea, however, to call the **McKinney Falls Swimming Hotline** (243-0848) first if you plan to swim.

Park office hours are 8 a.m. to 5 p.m. daily, while the gates remain open from 8 a.m. until 10 p.m. Take U.S. Highway 183 south to Scenic Loop Road, where you turn right. The park entrance is on Scenic Loop 2 miles west of U.S. Highway 183. Or take William Cannon east from IH 35; go right on Running Water, left on Colton-Bluff Springs Road, and left on McKinney Falls Parkway to the park entrance.

Monument Hill/Kreische Brewery (409/968-5658) is a state historical site with just 40 acres where visitors can enjoy a museum, trails, a playground, and picnics.

Mother Neff State Park (800/792-1112 or 817/853-2389) the oldest state park in Texas, is roughly 100 miles from Austin. Tall trees, shade, and relaxation await visitors to the 259 acres of this park. Picnic and camp in the beautiful Leon River bottom, also a great place for hiking. Campsites accommodate up to 8 persons. The nearest store is located 5 miles from the park. Bring your own firewood. Pets must be kept on a leash. Take IH 35 north to Temple. At Temple take Texas Highway 36 west, turn right at Texas Highway 236. After you cross Belton Lake the park will be on your left. The address is Route 1, Box 58, Moody, Texas, 76557.

Palmetto State Park (210/672-3266) is 55 miles south of Austin on U.S. Highway 183 past Luling; turn right on Park Road 11. Located along the San Marcos River in the post oak savannah vegetational region, the park is named for its abundant growth of dwarf palmetto plants. Three short nature trails and a primitive hiking trail provide a glimpse of wild irises, ferns, and other native species. The Ottine Swamp, within the park, has unusually luxuriant vegetation and sulphur springs. It has long drawn naturalists from all over the state.

West of Austin, several state parks offer different terrain from those to the east. At **Blanco State Park** (210/833-4333) a dam forms a seminatural pool that is great for swimming, especially for children. Picnics, too, are popular, and a group facility, showers, and hookups are available.

Pedernales Falls State Park (210/868-7304) is nestled in the Texas Hill Country about an hour from Austin. The Pedernales River drops 50 feet over stair steps of layered limestone. The park features fern-lined creeks, small canyons, huge bald cypress trees bordering the clear river, wildlife, and numerous primitive areas. Activities include swimming, boating, camping, and hiking. The 7.5-mile Wolf Mountain trail climbs to a high spot in the park with views of the Hill Country below. A 5-mile trail crosses to the east side of the river (fording is required) and passes the site of a pioneer cemetery. A short but beautiful half-mile nature trail gives explanations of the park's plant species and ends at an overlook above Twin Falls. Go 32 miles west of Austin on U.S. Highway 290; turn right on RM 3232, and go 7 miles.

There are 3 **State Wildlife Management Areas** nearby that serve a variety of functions. A small one, Old Tunnel, in the Fredericksburg area, is dedicated to protecting the tunnel's bat population. The Granger Management Area has 11,120 acres in Williamson County where restoring the prairie and salvaging the gene pool of grasses is the focus. Somerville, near Giddings, protects a variety of native flora and fauna on its 3,189 acres.

▮ Private Parks

Some lovely park areas near Austin are privately owned, such as **Krause Springs** (210/693-4181), a natural spot with swimming and "chutes" to slide down that delight children. Expect a fee. Take Texas Highway 71 west, cross the Pedernales River, go 7 miles, turn right on Spur 191 at the Exxon Station, right on County Road 404 and look for a sign on the left directing you to this private park.

Windy Point Park (250-1963), not to be confused with publicly owned Bob Wentz Park at Windy Point described previously, is great for picnics because it operates a food service on weekends. Its focus is scuba diving, but boating, swimming, sunbathing, and even volleyball are popular here, too. The owners rent sailboats, motor boats, rafts, and inner tubes, but no boats are allowed in the buoyed swimming area for the protection of the swimmers. (See Chapter 4, *In and on the Water,* under *Snorkeling and Scuba Diving,* for directions to this busy park on Lake Travis.)

A quiet, secluded setting on Lake Travis is **Camp Chautauqua** (264-1752), which is actually part of Pace Bend Recreation Area. Two deep-water coves make it perfect for swimming and canoeing. The name comes from Chautauquas, which were tent shows at the turn of the century that provided entertainment and education. With 4 covered open-air pavilions, the camp is ideal for picnics, retreats, and educational functions on water quality, water safety, or the environment. Besides camping, volleyball courts, a playground, and a ball field are offered.

Although owned by the Lower Colorado River Authority, Camp Chautauqua is operated by the Adopt-the-Colorado River Foundation, so it is listed here under private parks. Reservations are required. Pace Bend Recreation Area charges a fee to get into the park but waives this fee for persons with reservations at Camp Chautauqua, provided a deposit is sent in advance. The camp itself charges an entry fee, although children under 6 get in free. Expect additional fees, which vary depending upon the type of accommodations you reserve. Take Texas Highway 71 west to RM 2322, go north 4.6 miles to Pace Bend Recreation Area, and ask for directions to the camp at the park entrance.

▪ Park Passes and Reservations

For those who use the county and state park systems often during a year's time, a pass is a way to save money. Travis County has a yearly pass available at $50 per vehicle that exempts the holder from paying the $5 day-use entry fee at the parks and provides a $5 discount on camping fees.

The State of Texas offers two passports. The first is a Conservation Passport, which lasts for a year from the date of purchase and costs $25. The day-use entrance fee into a park is waived under this program. For information on purchasing a Texas Conservation Passport, call 800/792-1112, 8 a.m. to 5 p.m. Monday through

Friday. The second program is a Parkland Passport free to senior citizens 65 and older and to disabled veterans with a 60 percent or greater disability. The Parkland Passport provides to the holder a lifetime exemption from day-use entrance fees.

Reservations for group gatherings or campsites are generally made through the agency that manages the park or other facility that you want to use. Below is a list of handy phone numbers:

- Austin Parks and Recreation Department, 480-3036

- Travis County Parks Visitors Information and Reservations, 473-9437

- LCRA, 473-4083 or 800/776-5272 ext. 4083

- Texas Parks and Wildlife Department, 389-8900 for all State Park Reservations

▌ Running and Walking

Newcomers will find that Central Texas is paradise for runners and walkers. Whether you are interested in recreation, fitness, or competition, Austin offers plenty of opportunities.

A multitude of routes exist in Austin for those whose feet, knees and ankles are still fresh enough to run on pavement. One favorite begins at **Texas Memorial Stadium** on the UT campus and continues up Red River Street to the Hancock Golf Course, at 41st Street and Red River, returning to the stadium. Other neighborhoods that have proven runner-friendly include **Hyde Park**, **Allandale**, and **Tarrytown** in central Austin and **Travis Heights** south of the river.

For those runners and walkers whose joints and feet demand a softer surface, there are several options, the most popular of which is the **Town Lake Hike-and-Bike Trail.** Many people start at the MoPac foot bridge (either on the north side next to the Austin High School tennis court or on the south side at the Austin Nature Center parking lot). Another common starting point is the parking lot south of the river on 1st Street at **Auditorium Shores**, but there are several other spots along both sides of the river.

People in the north central part of the city often choose the track at **Camp Mabry**, a 1-mile loop just west of MoPac on 35th Street. Though not a lighted route, enough light comes from the highway traffic to allow safe running at night. Many who live in the southern part of the city prefer the track at **St. Edward's University**. Although this short loop, only a quarter of a mile long, creates some monotony, it is blessed with a magnificent view of the Austin skyline.

Seton Good Health School (323-1111) and the Austin Recreation Center (476-5662) provide classes in walking and jogging occasionally, and the University of Texas (471-5234) has regularly scheduled fitness courses that involve running or walking as well.

The Colorado River Walkers put on Volkswalks throughout the year, and the Austin Sierra Club meets regularly for a Sunday morning jog or walk around Town Lake at 8 a.m. at the Austin

TRAIL LOOPS DISTANCE IN MILES Kilometers = miles x .6214	BRIDGES					
	MOPAC	LAMAR	FIRST STREET	CONGRESS AVE.	IH 35	LONGHORN DAM
B MOPAC		2.9	4.1	4.5	6.9	10.1
R LAMAR	2.9		1.5	1.9	4.3	7.5
I **D** FIRST STREET	4.1	1.5		0.8	3.1	6.4
G CONGRESS AVE.	4.5	1.9	0.8		2.8	6.0
E IH 35	6.9	4.3	3.1	2.8		4.0
S LONGHORN DAM	10.1	7.5	6.4	6.0	4.0	

High School tennis court parking lot. The Austin Runners' Club has been serving the city's running community for over 15 years, with membership information available at Run-Tex, located at 919 West 12th Street. Run-Tex is the hub of activity for running and race walking events. This store is stocked not only with running shoes, clothes, and other equipment but also with application forms for runs, races, and race walks throughout Central Texas. Other sources of running and walking information are the Thursday "XL ent." section (see Escapes: Sporting Events) of the *Austin American-Statesman* and *Inside Texas Running*, a publication available at most sporting goods stores.

Races and fun runs of all lengths are scheduled throughout the year, but the King Kong of all events is the Capitol 10,000. A 10-kilometer race held every year in late March or early April, this is the largest run in Texas and one of the largest in the country. It comes complete with costumed runners, soldiers, politicians, and spectators. Other running events of note include the Bun Run and the Austin Sierra Club Earth Day Fun Run (5-kilometer runs held in the spring), the Daisy 5K (a race held in May for women only), the Republic of Texas Race Walk held in March, and the Decker Challenge, an 11-mile race in December. The annual Austin Motorola Marathon in early spring is a relative newcomer that seems to have become popular.

Bicycling

Longtime Austin residents often refer to Austin as the "center of the universe." From a cyclist's point of view, that's close to the truth, given its mild climate year-round. Austin offers a wide variety of cycling opportunities, because the Balcones Fault runs north-south through Austin. As a result, area bikers have ready access to two distinctly different bicycling experiences. In general, rides east of IH 35 are flat to rolling, while to the west riders are challenged by hills ranging from gentle slopes to the appropriately named Heart Break Hill on Lake Creek Road.

The best single guide to bicycling within the city is the *Austin Bicycle Map,* available at most bike shops. This map was produced by the Texas Bicycle Coalition (Box 1121, Austin, Texas, 78767, 476-7433) in cooperation with the city of Austin. It indicates cycling routes for riding around town, uses red lines to indicate "very difficult routes," and lists a set of 16 "Cycle Safety Tips," which include riding on the right side of the road and wearing a helmet always.

Several Austin bicycle shops rent bikes. Consult the yellow pages of the phone directory to find the one closest to you.

Listed below are a few of the most enjoyable in-town rides for those with sufficient riding skills to share space with motor vehicles:

Shoal Creek Boulevard provides an easy ride through tree-shaded residential neighborhoods. Shoal Creek runs north-south, parallel to and between Lamar Boulevard and MoPac. The south end of Shoal Creek is at West 38th Street by Seton Hospital. Its northern terminus is at Research Boulevard, east of the MoPac-U.S. Highway 183 interchange. To avoid the northern end of Shoal Creek, which is commercial rather than residential, riders can turn west at the 4-way stop at White Rock (the 6100 block), and then go

4 blocks and turn right on Great Northern. This will make their ride more car free. At the north end of Great Northern, riders can turn back south, or turn right on Foster and rejoin Shoal Creek. For riders coming from west of MoPac, there is access via the bike path running east from the intersection of Far West Boulevard and MoPac (suitable for touring and mountain bikes).

Loop 360 offers riding for cyclists who do not want to stop for traffic every couple of blocks. This divided highway has ample shoulders and provides a good workout without leaving the city. Starting from the north, Loop 360 runs from the Arboretum at the junction of Loop 360 and U.S. Highway 183 south to Brodie Oaks Shopping Center at the junction of Loop 360 and Lamar Boulevard (suitable for touring and mountain bikes).

The **Town Lake Hike-and-Bike Trail,** which circles Town Lake, is popular for off-road bicycling. For those arriving by car from the north, the most popular parking spot is the lot by Austin High School, under the bridge that carries MoPac over Town Lake. Those coming from the south by car can park in the lot west of the southern approach of the 1st Street Bridge over Town Lake.

Another popular off-road trail runs up **Barton Creek Greenbelt** from Zilker Park. This is much more challenging than the Town Lake Trail and involves several creek crossings. The trail runs upstream from the parking lot by the swimming pool. Sometimes this trail is closed after heavy rains or for maintenance. For late information on closings, call the **Trail Info-line**, 472-1267. The other major access point is the Loop 360 Access on the north side of the highway, between the Loop 360-MoPac intersection and the Loop 360-Lamar intersection.

Bee Caves Road west of Loop 360 provides a scenic 6.7-mile ride with spectacular views. Bee Caves Road, which becomes RM 2244, has wide shoulders for easy riding. The wide shoulders begin at Barton Creek Boulevard, which intersects Bee Caves Road 1.1 miles west of Loop 360. Closer to town Bee Caves has heavy traffic with no shoulders and is not recommended for riding.

The **Veloway**, located southeast of the intersection of MoPac and Slaughter Lane (behind Bowie High School), provides a unique biking experience. It looks like a paved 2-lane highway winding through the woods. The beauty of it is, no cars. The Veloway is a closed loop 3.1 miles long. To reach the main Veloway entrance, go 0.9 miles south of the MoPac-Slaughter intersection (4.6 miles south of the MoPac-U.S. Highway 290 intersection) and turn left. Cross the northbound lanes of MoPac and continue on for 0.2 miles to the parking area. The Veloway is open from dawn to dusk. All traffic goes clockwise.

Numerous groups organize rides in the Austin area. They have a good knowledge of the Austin area and can provide suggestions tailored to individual riders. The Austin Cycling Association (ACA) is the largest local biking club. Every Saturday and Sunday ACA organizes a short ride (roughly 25 miles) and a long one (roughly 50 miles) with a common starting point. Nonmembers are welcome. For information consult *Austin Cycling News* (available at most bike shops) or contact the Austin Cycling Association (Box 5993, Austin, Texas, 78763, 478-3065).

The Williamson County Cycling Club also organizes rides in the Austin area, offering a 15-20-mile ride each Saturday and a longer one on Sunday. In addition, it offers rides on Tuesday and Thursday afternoons. For more information call the club's sponsor, the Round Rock YMCA, at 244-1232 or 218-0879 outside regular office hours.

The Violet Crown Sports Association offers rides for faster riders. Weekend rides extend 45-60 miles for all members and 70-80 miles for racers. Their newsletter, which describes these activities, can be found in bike shops or they can be contacted at P.O. Box 3479, Austin, Texas, 78764. The Pedaler's Racing Club participates in bicycle races and stages training rides every Saturday and Sunday. For more information contact Don Hutchison at 441-0661.

The Austin Ridge Riders organize rides for experienced mountain bikers. Their rides are listed in the *Austin Cycling News*. The group can be reached at 454-2185. They also work to educate mountain bikers.

The University of Texas Cycling Club organizes rides that leave daily from the UT campus for lengths of 30 miles and up. Call UT Recreational Sports at 471-4003 for information on this group.

Some of the most popular rides outside Austin are described below.

The **Willow City Loop** provides magnificent views of the Hill

Country. While always enjoyable, this ride is spectacular when the bluebonnets are in bloom. When ridden as indicated below (counter-clockwise), you will go down one steep hill and then regain altitude on a steady, but gentle, upgrade on Texas Highway 16. To reach the loop, go to the Y intersection of U.S. Highway 290 and Texas Highway 71 in Oak Hill, take U.S. Highway 290 west for 33.7 miles, turn right on U.S. Highway 281, and continue north for 8.6 miles, passing through Johnson City on U.S. Highway 281. Turn left on FM 1323 and go 24.7 miles, passing through Sandy. The start is in Willow City.

START: Begin the ride by continuing north (the same direction as FM 1323 was headed before it turned left), with the GTE building to your left.

13.3	Turn left on Texas Highway 16.
19.2	Turn left on FM 1323.
22.0	FINISH

The **Blanco Ride** provides scenic views of hill country ranches. To reach the start, go to the Y intersection of U.S. Highway 290 and Texas Highway 71 in Oak Hill, take U.S. Highway 290 west for 33.7 miles, turn left on U.S. Highway 281, and continue south 8 miles to Blanco. Park on the side of the courthouse square opposite U.S. Highway 281. This ride is moderately hilly.

START: Ride north (in the direction of the post office) and turn right on 4th Street. Continue across Blanco River. Fourth Street becomes Loop 163.

1.8	Turn left on U.S. Highway 281.
2.2	Turn left on RM 32.
8.4	Turn right on RM 473.
14.2	Turn left on U.S. Highway 281, cross Little Blanco River.
14.3	Turn right on County Road 101.
19.8	Turn right at the unmarked T intersection (onto County Road 102).
26.2	Cross river and turn right at stop sign (onto Fulcher Street). Fulcher becomes Main Street.
26.7	Turn left on U.S. Highway 281.
27.0	Turn right 1 block before traffic light.
27.1	FINISH

To reach the start of the **Dripping Springs Ride**, go to the Y intersection of U.S. Highway 290 and Texas Highway 71 in Oak Hill, take U.S. Highway 290 14.3 miles west, pass the traffic light in Dripping Springs, and continue on U.S. Highway 290 0.4 miles. Turn right just past the large stone church across from the Diamond Shamrock gas station and park in the parking lot of the Dripping Springs Middle School.

START: Ride to and cross U.S. Highway 290. Turn left (toward traffic light).

0.05   Take the first right, County Road 190.
2.3   At Y continue right on County Road 190, across the low-water crossing.
8.8   At the unmarked intersection:
        a. you may return from here on the same route, for a total of 17.6 miles, or
        b. you may take a left on RM 165.
9.6   If you are continuing, turn left at County Road 165, which will loop back to RM 165.
15.4   At the unmarked intersection with RM 165, turn right, continue back to County Road 190 and return to Dripping Springs for a total of 24.2 miles.

The **Bastrop-Buescher Ride** provides a scenic view of the Lost Pines of Bastrop and Buescher State Parks. There are a few steep hills. However, even if you have to walk your bike up, the hills are so short they should not discourage you from taking this ride. It is recommended when spring wildflowers are in bloom. To reach the start of this ride, take Texas Highway 71 southeast from Austin. As you enter Bastrop on Texas Highway 71, turn left onto Loop 150 before reaching the Colorado River. Continue on Loop 150 past Main Street (first light past bridge). Turn right 1 block past Main Street, onto Water Street. Go 1 block and turn left onto Pine Street and park at the courthouse. While this ride can also begin in Bastrop State Park, starting at the courthouse avoids the auto entry fee. Or you can get a Conservation Passport, a good way not only to avoid the entry fee but also to support parks. Safety note: Some of the cattleguards on this ride have a space in the center through which a bike wheel can fall, so keep to the right when crossing them.

START: Follow Pine Street away from the Colorado River, crossing railroad tracks.

0.7	Turn left on divided highway.
0.8	Turn right on Loop 150, go up hill.
1.6	At Y intersection turn right on Loop 150, and then immediately leave Loop 150 and enter Bastrop State Park through stone entranceway to your left.
2.0	Pass park headquarters.
2.3	Turn left on Park Road 1A at monument to Felipe Enrique Neri, Baron de Bastrop.
2.8	Turn right on Park Road 1A.
3.5	Turn left at the water tank, continuing on Park Road 1C.
8.8	Cross 154, continue on Park Road 1C.
12.4	Continue past Science Park.
14.1	Turn left at stop sign, onto Park Road 1E.
15.1	Reach Buescher Park headquarters. Restrooms and soft drink machine are here.
15.2	Continue straight across FM 153.
16.0	Continue straight across divided road (Texas Highway 71), following power line.
17.0	Turn left at stop sign onto Texas Highway 95, cross Colorado River, and enter Smithville.
17.7	Turn right on FM 2571 before crossing railroad tracks.
24.4	Continue across railroad tracks at Upton.
27.7	Turn right on Texas Highway 304.
35.2	Turn right on Texas Highway 71.
35.4	Turn left on side road at the furniture store.
36.5	Turn left on Loop 150, crossing the river into Bastrop.
37.0	Turn right onto Water Street (1 block past light).
37.1	Ride ends at the courthouse.

McKinney Falls State Park has 2 magnificent bike venues. On the same side of Onion Creek as the Park Headquarters, there is a closed 3.5 mile loop (with an interior spur to the camping area). This paved path runs along cypress-lined Onion Creek and provides a view of the Upper Falls. The other side of the loop winds through higher land, passing woods and fields, which in the spring are replete with wildflowers.

The best parking for the loop is at the Visitor Center, which can be reached by driving 0.5 miles past Park Headquarters.

The other trail, Homestead Trail, can be reached by taking a right turn 0.1 miles past Park Headquarters and continuing a third of a mile to the end of the road. From the parking lot at end of the road, continue down to Onion Creek and cross it 40 feet above the falls. (Do not try riding your bike across, the stream bottom is quite slippery.) Continue up the dirt road which is visible on the opposite side of the creek. At the top of the rise, a trail sign will direct bikers in a clockwise direction down a single-track bike route. This 3.5-mile loop is more challenging than the other loop, crossing roots, rocks, and watercourses. Riders are literally in contact with nature, as the tall grasses brush bikers' legs. Most of the trail is through woods and fields. However, it does offer stark architectural contrasts. Riders can view the remains of the McKinney homestead, for which the trail is named, as well as the modern Texas Parks and Wildlife Headquarters, behind which the trail immediately passes.

Rocky Hill Ranch (512/237-3112) is a bicycle park for mountain bike riders to experience the same scenic countryside available to riders in Bastrop and Buescher State Parks. Jeep roads and single-lane tracks wend their way through the woods for 20 miles. Located on 1,200 acres, this working cattle ranch provides an opportunity for all levels of riders. Trails are rated, just like ski slopes, for beginning, intermediate, and advanced riders. The ranch, which was opened to riders in 1992, is still developing programs and facilities. Bring your own bikes; no rentals are available. As of now it is strictly B.Y.O.B. (bring your own bike), but plans are to rent bikes and to combine bike rides with river trips.

Rocky Hill Ranch is open Thursday through Sunday from 9 a.m. until about 1 hour prior to dusk. (Call ahead after heavy rains.) Primitive camping facilities are available, together with bathroom and shower facilities at Ranch Headquarters, for those who want to spend the night. Group rates and season passes are available. Approved helmets are required. To reach the ranch, take Texas Highway 71 southeast past Bastrop to the Smithville exit. Immediately after exiting, turn left on FM 153, pass the entrance to Buescher State Park, and continue on FM 153 for exactly 2 more miles. Then turn left through a gateway adorned with a yellow bicycle.

Camping and Backpacking

Ah, cooking over a campfire, sleeping under the stars, dipping water out of a rushing stream, no one else within hearing distance. Well, not quite in Central Texas. Unless you use a designated fire ring in a state park, ground fires are discouraged, in our dry climate, if not downright forbidden. And since gathering wood is prohibited, you have to bring your own wood anyway. High morning humidity almost guarantees a heavy morning dew to dampen sleeping bags and spirits, and streams in Texas are not potable, so backpackers have to carry any water they use. As for solitude, Texas ranks near the bottom of all the states in recreational land, and few large tracts of public wilderness are available to campers.

But you can enjoy camping or backpacking in Texas by keeping in mind some of our special circumstances. Central Texas has several state parks, most on water, as well as many county, LCRA, and private campgrounds with facilities for both car camping and primitive camping. Here are a few of the most scenic and popular. Please note that all forbid ground fires except in barbecue pits, and

no collection of firewood is allowed. (See Chapter 2, A*t the Park,* for directions to state parks.)

Both **Bastrop State Park** and **Buescher State Park** are relatively small, but Bastrop in particular is amenable to hiking. The trail crosses several creeks, passes 2 former stock ponds that are now home to frogs and water fowl, and meanders over ridges and through swales with varied plant and animal communities. Primitive camping is allowed on the hiking trail. Both parks have campsites with or without RV hookups. Buescher has screened shelters and Bastrop has wonderful rock cabins built in the 1930s. Since the cabins are extremely popular, make your reservations early but not more than 90 days in advance (the maximum allowed).

Pedernales Falls State Park, about 45 minutes west of Austin, has some of the nicest car camping sites around. Most are well screened from one another and afford plenty of shade. Besides the massive falls area, which is often deserted in the morning until around 10 a.m., the park offers a trail along the river, a nature trail above Twin Falls, and 7 miles of hiking trail. Primitive camping is allowed in a designated area along the trail about a mile from the parking area. This trail was laid out and built by the Sierra Club during the initial development of the park in the early 1970s.

Enchanted Rock State Natural Area, 2 hours northwest of Austin, has walk-in car camping sites, which are very close together but do have shade shelters. The main attraction here, of course, is the rock itself, the largest granite dome west of the Mississippi, and second only in size to Georgia's Stone Mountain. A trail from the campground leads to the top of the 325-foot-high dome and down again, and another trail around the "back" of the rock leads to 60 primitive camping sites with composting toilets.

About 3 hours southwest of Austin is the **Hill Country State Natural Area**, donated to the state with the proviso that it be "kept untouched by modern civilization, with everything preserved intact." Camping is primitive in a 100-acre area at the end of a 2.5 mile trail. The only amenities are a chemical toilet and a water faucet at the parking lot. Hill Country is especially popular with horseback riders, offering 2 marked equestrian trails.

Inks Lake State Park, 1.5 hours northwest of Austin, has 207 car-camping sites, 22 screen shelters, and primitive camping a mile down the hiking trail (but not on the lake). Reserve a campsite well in advance, because the beauty of this park makes it extremely popular. It's the ideal setting for a relaxed weekend away from home if you don't have a burning need for solitude.

Years ago, backpacking meant camping with minimal heavy gear, and the strongest back carried the most equipment. Modern technology and space-age materials have reduced the load to such a degree that today even children can carry their fair share of the gear for a multiday trip. Whole Earth Provision Company, REI (Recreational Equipment, Inc.), and Wilderness Supply all carry a wide assortment of specialized equipment, from tents, clothing, and sleeping bags to cookstoves, nesting pots, and water purifiers. All three stores have knowledgeable, helpful staff who enjoy using the equipment they sell. In addition to these sources of how-to and with-what information, UT Recreational Sports and the Sierra Club offer occasional workshops or courses on backpacking. Tips, short-cuts, and menu ideas can be gleaned that will make it much more pleasant to carry your household on your back.

PUBLICATIONS

Axcell, Claudia. *Simple Foods for the Pack*. San Francisco, California: Sierra Club Books, 1986.

Fletcher, Colin. *Complete Walker III*. New York, New York: Knopf, 1984. Another classic by a man who has "walked through time" (the Grand Canyon), sparking a nationwide interest in hiking and backpacking in the early 1970s

Little, Mickey. *Camper's Guide to Texas Parks, Lakes, and Forests*. Houston, Texas: Gulf Publishing, Lone Star Books, 1990. This is the 3rd ed. first comprehensive list (with park maps) of the state's camping resources. The state is divided into 4 regions, and camp-grounds are listed by region.
———. *Hiking and Backpacking Trails of Texas*. Houston, Texas: Gulf Publishing, Lone Star Books, 1990. A good companion to Mickey's camper's guide.

Manning, Harvey. *Backpacking One Step at a Time*. New York, New York: Random House, 1986. A classic resource of how-tos and equipment.

Miller, George O., and Delena Tull. *Texas Parks and Campgrounds*. Houston, Texas: Gulf Publishing, Lone Star Books, 1990. An alphabetical listing of state and national parks, national forests, and U.S. Corps of Engineers parks with public camping facilities, as well as some noncommercial and concession-operated campgrounds.

San Diego Chapter of the Sierra Club. *Wilderness Basics*. Sea
Washington: Mountaineers, 1993.

■ Caving

Thanks to the Balcones Fault, Austin lies in the heart of one of the
major caving regions of the country. The fault was named by
Spanish explorers who felt the hills west of Austin looked like
balconies, so gave it the name "Balcones," Spanish for balconies.
The fault uplifted the Edwards limestone some 50 million years
ago. Through the millennia water percolated through the limestone
and carved out numerous caves.

Anyone entering caves should have a sturdy hard hat and multiple
light sources. A single flash-
light will not do.
Solo caving is not
recommended since
a call for help from
underground may
never be heard.

Some 200 caves
exist in Travis
County alone.
They lack the
spectacular size of
Carlsbad Cav-
erns, but what
they lack in size
and formations
is made up for
by their unique
fauna. Some 44
cave-adapted
species are found
in Travis County
caves, 5 of which
are listed by the
Environmental
Protection Agency as

…es. One small cave, **Tooth Cave**, has 12 cave-
more than Mammoth Cave in Kentucky.

are on private property and require owners' per-
. However, 2 are on public land. One of these is the
on top of Enchanted Rock. It has a prominent
entrance visible from the top. The other cave on public land is
Airman's Cave which is 11,000 feet long, the longest in Travis
County. It runs under Lamar Boulevard. There is an entrance to
this cave on Barton Creek, about 3/4 of a mile downstream from the
Loop 360 bridge. To find the cave, walk to the electric transmission
lines about a mile below the bridge. Then walk upstream. As you
face upstream, the cave will be on your left. Go upstream about
400 feet until you see some large flat boulders, about 20 feet across,
piled on top of each other at stream level. The cave is on the bank
about 30 feet downstream and 15 feet above the boulders.

Those wanting a more varied caving experience are encouraged to
contact the University of Texas Speleological Society, which meets
on the UT campus in Painter Hall, Room 2.48 at 7:30 p.m. on the
first and third Wednesdays of the month. Interested persons can
also contact veteran caver Bill Russell at 453-4774.

The outstanding commercial cave in the Austin area is **Natural
Bridge Caverns** (210/651-6101), with its large passages and
massive formations. It can be reached by taking FM 1863 12 miles
west of New Braunfels, and then turning south on FM 3009 for
3.5 miles. Beginning at 9 a.m., tours leave every 30 minutes. The
last tour leaves at 6 p.m. from June through August and at 4 p.m.
in other months.

Inner Space (512/863-5545) is the commercial cave closest to
Austin, discovered when the Highway Department was drilling
cores for an interchange on IH 35. The cave features its own sound-
and-light program. The hours at Inner Space are 10 a.m. to 5 p.m.
in winter and 9 a.m. to 6 p.m. in summer (Memorial Day through
Labor Day). To reach the cave simply turn off IH 35 at exit 259, just
north of Georgetown.

Cave without a Name (210/537-4212), also known as **Century
Cave**, is located near Boerne. It is about as close to visiting an
undeveloped cave as you can get and still have a guide. To get to
the cave go to the Y intersection of U.S. Highway 290 and Texas

Highway 71 in Oak Hill, take U.S. Highway 290 west for 33.7 miles, turn left on U.S. Highway 281 and continue for 17.1 miles, passing through Blanco and crossing the Little Blanco River. Then turn right on RM 473 and continue for 15.3 miles, passing Kendalia. Then take a left on FM 474 and continue for 9.7 miles, crossing the Guadalupe River. Turn left on Kreutzberg Road, and continue for 3.6 miles. A sign will direct you to turn right onto a gravel road. Continue for a mile until you reach the cave.

Another cave near Boerne is **Cascade Caverns** (210/755-8080), which has its own waterfall. To reach the cave leave I 10 at Exit 543 (14 miles northwest of San Antonio). Signs will direct you the remaining three miles to the cave. Hours are 10 a.m. to 4 p.m.

Longhorn Cavern (512/756-6976) near Burnet has a colorful history, including use as a saloon during prohibition. The cave is in a state park, which has an attractive WPA-built stone building. To reach the cave, drive five miles south of Burnet on U.S. Highway 281. There a sign will direct you to turn right to the cave. There are tours at 10:30 a.m., 1 p.m., and 3 p.m. on weekdays in the winter. During the winter weekends and every day in the summer, there is a tour every hour, 9 a.m. to 5 p.m.

◼ Rock Climbing

Central Texas is a great place for rock climbing. Difficulty can range from an easier 5.6 rating to a rather difficult 5.12 or 5.13. Levels here vary from excellent limestone crags to a premium granite climb up sheer rock just 90 miles from Austin.

Because of inherent risks, a beginner should go with an experienced guide or take a rock climbing class. Mountain Madness (443-5854) and Texas Mountain Guides (482-9208) are 2 professional guides that offer both private instruction and classes. UT Recreational Sports (471-1093) offers classes several times a semester, and the **Austin Nature Center** (327-8180) may offer classes in rock climbing and rappelling as well. Equipment can be purchased at Whole Earth Provision and Wilderness Supply, as well as REI where you can see "the rock" as you walk in the door. These stores may also have suggestions for climbing.

There are at least 2 climbing clubs in Austin. One is the University of Texas Climbing Club, which meets on the second and fourth Thursday of each month, 8 p.m. to 10 p.m., at Painter Hall, 24th and University Avenue, north of the Main Building, in Room 2.48. For more information, call Campus Activities (471-3065). Another climbing club is Central Texas Mountaineers (CTM), which meets on the first Thursday of each month at 7:30 p.m. at Pseudo Rock, 200 Trinity Street. For more information, call Pseudo Rock at 474-4376 or Barry Wilson at 447-9132.

Bouldering sites include the **Sunken Gardens** in Zilker Park (behind the baseball fields off Robert E. Lee Road) and the **Waller Creek Bridge** at San Jacinto and Martin Luther King Boulevard. Another spot where you need only shoes and a chalk bag is the bouldering rock at **Bull Creek Park**. From MoPac take RM 2222 west to just past the County Line Restaurant, go right on Lakewood Drive (you've gone too far if you get to Loop 360), and park in the dirt parking lot on the right just before the low-water crossing. Walk between the basketball court and picnic area to the rock marked "bouldering site." Or if you prefer routes, park on the other side of the low-water crossing and walk back down toward the crossing where, on the right (facing south), is a small trail leading to routes rated 5.11–5.13. Although the climb is usually wet because the rock seeps, it is shaded most of the day.

Equally close in are the limestone routes along the **Barton Creek Greenbelt**, where you will need a rope and other gear. Most of the climbing takes place on the north side of Barton Creek between the Gus Fruh Access (on the south side of the creek across the street from 2631 Barton Hills Drive) and the Spyglass Access (on the north side of the creek).

Farther out **Milton Reimers Fishing Ranch**, near Hamilton Pool, features routes rated 5.6–5.13, most of which can be top-roped. The routes are well protected, and the rock quality may be the best in Austin. Open every day except Thursday, this remote, private place used to allow camping but not anymore, so keep it clean. Take Southwest Parkway west, turn right onto Texas Highway 71 (going north), and left on RM 3238 (Hamilton Pool Road). After about 15 miles, look for a gate and sign on the right. Pull in, stay to the left, and drive up to the house. Someone will greet you. Expect a fee.

Rock climbing groups routinely make trips to **Enchanted Rock**, which affords the only granite routes in Central Texas. It is located about 90 miles northwest of Austin off RM 965 between Llano and Fredericksburg. For more information consult *The Dome Driver's Manual* listed below. For information on other limestone crags around Austin, refer to *Central Texas Limestone,* also listed below. The best way to learn about them is from other rock climbers.

PUBLICATIONS

Crump, James, Robert Price, and Scott Harris. *The Dome Driver's Manual: A Climbers Guide to Enchanted Rock.* Austin, Texas: Big Fun Publications, 1990.

Jackson, Jeff, and Kevin Gallagher. *Central Texas Limestone: A Climber's Guide.* Austin, Texas: Homo Aggro Press, 1992.

Long, John. *Climbing Anchors*. Evergreen, Colorado: Chockstone Press, 1993.
————. *How to Face Climb*. Evergreen, Colorado: Chockstone Press, 1993.
————. *How to Rock Climb*. Evergreen, Colorado: Chockstone Press, 1993.

■ Archery

Archery is a quiet sport, centering around muscle control and concentration on the draw, anchoring, precise release, and follow-through. It is a relaxing mental and physical activity for all, including those in wheelchairs. To use the standard bow, the archer must develop muscle coordination, especially in the back and arms. The newer compound bow requires less strength while anchoring and aiming, leading to tighter competition between people of all ages and sizes.

The traditional style of archery—called field archery—utilizes a 2-dimensional target, such as the familiar bull's-eye, on an indoor or outdoor range. In recent years, the 3-D style has become popular, in which archers walk a course or path through natural habitat, stopping at designated spots along the trail to shoot at realistic, 3-dimensional targets simulating game animals. This approach combines a pleasant walk in the woods or fields with archery practice or competition. In Central Texas today, 3-D enthusiasts may well outnumber traditionalists.

Local clubs promote both styles, sponsoring regular competitions, and several area archers have competed at the state or national level. Both the International Field Archers Association (traditional) and the International Bowhunters Association (3-D), which sanction competition at local, national, and international levels, are well represented in Austin. There's lots of relaxed Sunday-afternoon target practice with family and friends, too. Members of the University of Texas Archery Sports Club—open to UT students, faculty, and staff—participate in intercollegiate competition.

Local clubs invite people to "come out and shoot" a time or two, meet the members, and check out the ranges. Archery ranges are located on unimproved land and may be primitive, with no running water or restrooms. Accessibility for people with disabilities is often limited because of rugged terrain and lack of amenities but not impossible for rugged individuals. Clubs lock the entrance gates to ranges but provide keys to members.

The Austin Archery Club meets in the "clubhouse," a pavilion on their range, at 6 p.m. on the first Monday of each month. Although the range is rocky, the practice range is flat enough for wheelchairs. Chemical toilets are on-site. Tournaments or "shoots" are held on the second Sunday of each month, February-September. There are annual dues, visitors may participate for a fee. To reach the range, take RM 2222, drive out City Park Road for about 3 miles, and turn in at the sign to the range.

The Williamson County Archery Club meets at 2 p.m. on the fourth Sunday of each month, January-September. The business meeting follows the "shoot." Members meet at the club's wooded, 40-acre range on IH 35 just north of Round Rock. The range occupies the southwest corner of IH 35 and RM 1431, and a mailbox at the gate has membership forms. Many members practice on Wednesday evenings. Although the range is accessible for people with disabilities, the "restroom" is the quaint, old-fashioned kind—an outhouse. WCAA sponsors a lot of family and youth activities. Annual dues.

The Chisholm Trail Bowhunters Association meets at 7 p.m. on the third Thursday of every month, February-December, in Belton at the Hallmark Restaurant (817/939-1920), 600 Forest Drive, off IH 35 at 6th Street. Bowhunting tournaments are held at 2 p.m. on the first Sunday of each month at the club range in Salado. Take IH 35 north to the Stillhouse exit and go north along the access road a short distance. Turn in at the sign on the gate, which displays the names and phone numbers of the club's officers. The CTBA emphasizes bowhunting with a range that has 28 3-D targets. The Association charges annual dues.

Archery Country (452-1222) offers lessons, league shooting, and a junior program. Open 10:30 a.m. to 8:30 p.m. Monday-Friday and 10 a.m. to 6 p.m. Saturday. Charges are by the hour. The address is 8910 Research Boulevard, Austin, Texas, 78758.

K C's Outdoors (288-6001) in Oak Hill invites archers to "walk in and shoot." Open 8 a.m. to 7 p.m. Monday-Thursday and Saturday, 8 a.m. to 8 p.m. on Friday, and 9 a.m. to 5 p.m. on Sunday. The address is 6800 West Highway 290, Austin, Texas, 78735.

General sporting-goods stores, listed in the telephone directory Yellow Pages, carry archery equipment and supplies, but the best selection and most knowledgeable salespeople can be found in archery specialty stores. Look for them under *Archery Equipment and Supplies* in the Yellow Pages. They repair equipment and disseminate information on local clubs and activities. Before you buy equipment, visit a club to learn about different kinds of bows and arrows. Did you know, for example, that aluminum arrows are safer than wooden ones? All the clubs hold special events, such as barbecues, tournaments, and youth and children's programs.

IN
AND ON
THE WATER

4

■ Swimming

In Austin and at points nearby, swimming is popular year-round because the climate is warm. Natural and seminatural spots abound, drawing swimmers, bathers, toe-tippers, and sunbathers to their shores. Since most of the areas do not have lifeguards, swimming is at your own risk. The City of Austin operates numerous swimming pools in the summer months. For hours of operation and other types of information on any of the city's pools, call the Austin Parks and Recreation Department's Aquatics Division at 476-4521. There are numerous swimming spots, several are outstanding.

You can swim for fitness year-round in the lanes at Stacy Pool and the open expanses of Barton Springs Pool. During swimming season all 6 municipal pools have lane lines open all day, and the 27 neighborhood pools have lane lines available sometime during the day. Swimming classes are held morning and evening at 11 pools. In 1994 5,000 children had lessons. Call PARD, 476-4521, for information on neighborhood pools and summer swimming classes and hours of operation.

In Zilker Park, just off Barton Springs Road, **Barton Springs Pool** is one of Austin's famous landmarks and easily the most popular swimming hole in the city. Spring fed and over 900 feet long, the pool was formed when Barton Creek was dammed up, so it has a natural rock and gravel bottom. There are varying depths, diving boards, and stairs and ladders for entry. The water temperature averages 68° F throughout the year, so enter the pool gingerly. As you swim across, feel how some spots are colder than others. A more refreshing swim is hard to find, but the pool is often crowded, especially on summer weekends. In recent years, the city has closed the pool when the fecal coliform count was high and posed a threat to swimmers, often the case after a heavy rain. To find out if the pool is open before traveling to the site, call the **hotline number** 867-3080, which operates 24 hours a day.

Fees are collected after 9 a.m. during the summer only. Pool doors open early at 5 a.m. From Lamar Boulevard, drive west on Barton Springs Road. At Robert E. Lee Drive, you have two options. You may turn left onto Robert E. Lee, go up a hill for about a quarter of a mile, and just past a baseball field turn into a gravel parking area on the right, which accesses the rear entrance to the pool. Alternatively, you may continue straight past Robert E. Lee, crossing the Barton Creek bridge. About a quarter of a mile past the bridge on the left is the main entrance to the pool and picnic area.

At certain times of the year when creek levels are high (but not too high), people flock to several swimming holes along Barton Creek. About a mile upstream from Barton Springs Pool where the creek runs roughly from west to east, **Campbell's Hole** appeals to crowds, as does **Gus Fruh Pool**, which is about another mile farther up the creek. Upstream from Gus Fruh, the creek bends around, passes under a Loop 360 bridge, reaches its southernmost point, and then turns north, passing under MoPac Boulevard. Not too much farther upstream from MoPac is **Twin Falls**, another well-known swimming hole, and yet another mile upstream is **Sculpture Falls**, where the creek runs roughly from north to south. There is another, more secluded swimming hole before you come to the end of the Barton Creek Greenbelt (see Chapter 1, *In the Heart of the City,* for points of access to this greenbelt). Hiking to this spot via the greenbelt is encouraged, but if necessary, it can be reached by taking Loop 360 and turning west onto Scottish Woods Trail, which dead-ends at Camp Craft Road. Space is tight here, so obey the parking signs for the sake of the neighborhood. The trailhead is on Camp Craft Road, and the trail down to the creek is steep and rugged.

Second only to Barton Springs Pool in popularity is **Deep Eddy Pool**, located just west of MoPac off Lake Austin Boulevard. On the south side of Lake Austin Boulevard, a little road takes you to both Deep Eddy Pool and Eilers Park. Deep Eddy is large with essentially three sections: the deep end is for diving, the middle for fitness swimming, and the rest of the pool slopes from 3 feet deep to a shallow wading area for toddlers.

For swimming enthusiasts who prefer warm water in the winter, an indoor heated pool at **St. Edward's University** is operated by the city and the university throughout the year, except during the few weeks in July and August when the Dallas Cowboys train at St. Ed's. The average pool temperature is 80°F. The pool is available to the public in the mornings, usually 7 a.m. to 11 a.m. weekdays and 8 a.m. to noon weekends. Call the city at 476-4521 (Aquatics) to make sure the times are still the same.

At **Stacy Pool**, located in Stacy Park at 700 East Live Oak Street, the water temperature in winter varies between 78 and 82°F. Each week the water in the pool is drained and filled from a warm aquifer. In the summer the water is changed on Mondays. In the winter, Saturday is used for the draining and refilling. Therefore, the temperature is likely to be warmer early in the week and cooler later on. There is no fee for swimming in this pool. To swim on the east side of town at Decker Lake, go to **Walter E. Long Metropolitan Park**, a city-owned park. It offers a small beach of coarse sand and lots of grass for sunning. The water, mostly shallow, is ideal for children. Take Decker Lane, turn east on Decker Lake Road, and go 1.5 miles to reach the park. Expect a fee.

Emma Long Metropolitan Park, also known as City Park or Lake Austin Metro Park, is a popular summer spot situated on a narrow stretch of Lake Austin. Water access is from a grassy bank or a wooden dock provided in a deeper area. There is a roped-off area for swimming and water play. Lifeguards are on duty, 12 noon to 6 p.m. on weekends only, Memorial Day through Labor Day. Children must be supervised when the lifeguard is not on duty. By city ordinance, *no swimming past 50 feet from shoreline*. Hours are 7 a.m. to 10 p.m. Head west on RM 2222. Half a mile past Loop 360 turn left onto City Park Road. Follow this road for 6.5 miles to the lake front.

Another unique swimming spot is **Hamilton Pool**, featuring a 65-foot waterfall for swimmers and hikers to enjoy. The pool and grotto were formed when the dome of an underground river collapsed thousands of years ago. Normal hours of operation are 9 a.m. to 6 p.m., but the park closes temporarily when all 100 spaces are taken in the parking lot or when the bacteria count is too high, so call 264-2740 in advance to make sure it is open. Take Texas Highway 71 west. About a mile past RM 620, turn left onto RM 3238 (Hamilton Pool Road), and go 13 miles to reach this treasure.

Selma Hughes Park, located about 2 miles east of Mansfield Dam, has a huge old live oak tree overhanging the water, complete with a rope swing. Water access is from a long grassy bank. There is no fee to use this park. Take RM 2222 west, turn left onto RM 620 and go about 2 miles, then turn left (south) onto Quinlan Park Road; after 4 or 5 miles, turn left onto Selma Hughes Park Road, and drive another mile or so to reach the park.

Hippie Hollow Park (McGregor Park), located off RM 620 2.5 miles down Comanche Trail, is unique because bathing suits are optional. The swimming is excellent, and sunbathing on the rocks or in the water on rafts is unmatched. Water access is steep and rocky. The water is deep in most places, and there are a number of high diving rocks. This Lake Travis park is usually quite crowded in summer, and boatloads of gawkers can become a nuisance as well as a danger to swimmers and sunbathers on rafts. In the past, Hippie Hollow has acquired a rather seedy reputation for drugs, theft, open sexual activity, and other similar problems. Despite its reputation, the atmosphere is generally laid back and pleasant. Expect a fee.

Mansfield Dam Recreation Area, at the west end of the dam off RM 620 on Lake Travis, is a popular spot for swimmers. A rocky point extends out into the water, dividing the open lake on one side from a cove on the other. It is in the cove where the swimming is most outstanding. Water access is achieved mostly by making one's way down a rocky terrain, but the hike is not that difficult. The depth drops off rapidly, but there's plenty of wading room. On summer weekends, this park, which has an entrance fee, can be very crowded.

Besides Hippie Hollow and Mansfield Dam, other parks on Lake Travis, owned by the Lower Colorado River Authority and managed by Travis County, offer swimming. These parks are **Arkansas Bend, Cypress Creek, Pace Bend, Sandy Creek,** and **Bob Wentz Park at Windy Point**. (See Chapter 2, *At the Park,* for more information on these LCRA parks.)

■ Canoeing, Kayaking, Rafting and Tubing

Diversity best describes the rivers and streams of Texas. The slow-moving, meandering, and deep waters of the coastal plains afford great scenic float trips, while the rapids and waterfalls of Hill Country rivers provide excitement and challenge. Many of the best streams in the state are within an hour or 2 of Austin, where canoeing, rafting, and tubing are popular activities. Local or regional organizations offer canoeing instruction and guided river trips, and rental and sales outlets supply the necessary equipment.

Normal flows feature rapids varying from mild Class Is to moderateClass IIIs. All rivers discussed here are best for *experienced* kayakers during periods of high water. For kayakers, the best areas during higher flow periods are the lower Guadalupe, Barton Creek, and the Pedernales. At flood stage, *all* Texas rivers can be killers.

Rivers and Rapids (formerly titled *Texas Rivers and Rapids*) is the best guidebook about floating Texas rivers. Available in most book stores or wilderness supply shops, this guide covers not only rivers in Texas but also rivers in Oklahoma and Arkansas. For information from Texas Parks and Wildlife on floating Texas rivers, call 800/792-1112.

RIVERS

The **Colorado River** was almost lost to recreation. The river was used as a dumping ground for sewage disposal in Austin until 1984 when the Sierra Club and other organizations sued the city, forcing a cleanup of sewage operations. By 1990 the river had regained most of its clarity and beauty once again and the many creeks along the Town Lake section are, picturesque and beautiful. With sand, gravel, or rock bottom, the river has many gravel bars and islands that make excellent campsites. The sections to consider running are:

- from U.S. Highway 190 northwest of Lampasas to Colorado Bend State Park, 29.8 miles

- from U.S. Highway 183 in southeast Austin to Bastrop, 50 miles

- from Bastrop to Smithville, 26.2 miles

- from Smithville to La Grange, 36.2 miles

Most of these runs are scenic and you can enjoy them almost any time of year, but allow yourself plenty of time. For more information on the Colorado, call Colorado River Longhorn Canoe at 409/732-3723 or the Lower Colorado River Authority at 473-4083 or 800/776-5272 ext. 4083.

Barton Creek is Austin's favorite waterway. It is one of the most glorious natural treasures found in any city, and the greenbelt along the creek is an oasis of flora, fauna, and natural beauty. At flood stage, Barton Creek below Loop 360 is one of the most exciting white water runs in the state. Before you make your plans check on the water level. Sometimes the creek is dry. For the latest river flows, contact LCRA at 473-3333. Different boats and tubes require different amounts of water. Kayaks usually need at least 200 cubic feet per second (cfs), while tubes can float at just 50 cfs. See the *Austin Chronicle's* "Barton Creek Guide" for complete information.

Canoeing the 12 mile stretch of Barton Creek from Highway 71 down to Lost Creek requires some experience. There are many strainers and low hanging branches over narrow channels and some remnants of fences across the creek. Allow plenty of time (5-7 hours at normal flow): private property on both banks means that you can't bail out if you lose daylight. There are 5 low-water dams. Carry your canoe to the left around the first 4 dams (watch for a protruding pipe at the fourth). Carry to the right around the fifth dam. By comparison, this section is more difficult than the San Marcos River. Take Texas Highway 71 west beyond Oak Hill and a little past Southwest Parkway. You will need to arrange for someone to drop you off because parking is not allowed here. Enter the creek from the southwest side of the bridge.

The **San Marcos River** starts in downtown San Marcos, just 40 miles from Austin, and flows directly from Aquarena Springs. Water flow, which is constant, is good to excellent, and the temperature is a tolerable 72 degrees year round. You will see lush, almost tropical vegetation, including elephant ears, water hyacinths, and canna lilies. There are several good rapids. You may get wet because of the swift narrow channels with overhanging limbs, downed trees, and small log jams. Certain spots like Cottonseed Rapids, are tricky for the novice, and there are some dams to portage and low bridges so be careful. You can always carry your canoe on land past a rough spot but be aware that there are ongoing issues with property owners. See *Rivers and Rapids* for detailed information on the rapids and suggested routes to run the river.

From Austin take IH 35 south; take the exit to Aquarena Springs Road (Loop 82) and head west; turn left on Bugg Lane, and then right to **City Park**. A concrete ramp provides easy access to the water. Alternate launch points are where County Road 101 crosses

County Road 266 at 5.5 miles, **Pecan Park Retreat** at 6.2 miles, **Sculls Crossing** at 9.2 miles, the low-water crossing below **Martindale Dam**, and Spencer Canoes at **Shady Grove Campground** at 11.5 miles. All of these mile references correspond with river maps found in *Rivers and Rapids*. Any of the put-in spots are also good take-out points, but the last take-out point for this section of the river is immediately below the FM 1977 crossing, east of Staples. For information, call T G Canoe Rental at 512/353-3946, Pecan Park Retreat at 512/392-6171, or Spencer Canoes at 512/357-6113. Pecan Park and Spencer Canoes both have good private campgrounds where river-front camping, water, showers, and electricity are available for a fee.

New Braunfels is known for its tubing on the **Comal River** and a water amusement park called **Schlitterbahn**, at 400 N. Liberty. Although Schlitterbahn is on the banks of the Comal River, you actually tube down man-made chutes and slides. Besides being highly developed, it is also expensive, so tubing down the river itself may be more to your liking.

The **Guadalupe River,** from FM 306 to New Braunfels, is the most popular stretch of river in the state. Its white water, scenic beauty, and proximity to large metropolitan areas downstream from Canyon Dam make it a favorite with river runners. This 20-mile stretch of the Guadalupe River can easily be divided into short trips 1-5 hours long, with many small, fun rapids and deep pools. Although the river has a few old weir dams, just look for notches in these dams. When in doubt about where to run a dam or rapid, get out and scout it; in other words, examine it from the shore and plan your run. Remember, you can always portage or walk around any spot that you are not sure you can do.

When you reach the bridge labeled "first crossing" start paying attention! **Hueco Springs Rapid**, **Slumber Falls**, and **Rock Garden Rapid**, which has cypress trees and a rock garden, will all challenge the novice. Run this stretch of the river only if you are a good swimmer, and always wear a life jacket. Check with outfitters for up-to-date water levels and safety information. At water levels above 500 cfs, you will need good boating skills.

From Austin take IH 35 south to the Canyon Lake/FM 306 exit. Go west on FM 306 approximately 20 miles to FM 2673. At this intersection you will find many outfitters, such as Whitewater Sports. You can also turn south onto FM 2673 and go 1 mile to River Road, which is one of the most scenic roads in the area, as it follows the river for 22 miles into New Braunfels. Look for the sign to Rio Raft Company, a river outfitter off River Road.

You can reach the lower end of River Road by taking IH 35 from Austin to the Texas Highway 46/New Braunfels exit. Turn right, go 4 miles on Texas Highway 46, turn right onto Gruene Road, and go 1 mile to the bridge, where outfitters are found on both sides of the road, such as Rockin 'R' River Rides and Gruene River Raft Company. Texas Canoe Trails also has camping along River Road.

With no private access to the Guadalupe River, it is best to use outfitters to access the river. Expect to pay about $10-$15 per person for a canoe or raft trip, with usually 2 people to a canoe, and 2, 4, or 6 people on a raft. There is a $20-$50 deposit on all canoes and rafts. If you have your own canoe, raft, or tube, expect to pay $3-$10 for parking and shuttle service. This is sometimes negotiable, depending on how busy the outfitters are.

Tubing is popular on this stretch of the river also, but be extremely careful tubing the lower 6 miles of the Guadalupe River where the rapids can be dangerous at certain water levels. You must swim well to tube this section of the river. Remember, you can walk around anything that looks dangerous to you. Ask an outfitter for safety instructions before tubing any section of the river.

The **Upper Guadalupe River**, 75 miles from Austin, is less crowded and the most scenic part of the Guadalupe. Several good access points along this section make it easy to break into a number of short, fun floats. Outfitters can recommend the stretch of the Upper Guadalupe that might be best for your skill level. Take IH 35 south to the Texas Highway 46/New Braunfels Exit and turn right to go west on Texas Highway 46. After 6 miles, you will veer off to the right and continue on Texas Highway 46. After another 16 miles or so, veer off to the right to get on FM 311 and go about 5 miles on FM 311 to **Big Foot Canoe**, which serves the entire length of the Upper Guadalupe River. The headquarters is a museum in its own right and worth the drive to see it. For more information call 210/885-7106.

Guadalupe River State Park is right on the Guadalupe River. To reach the park, take IH 35 south, go 18 miles west on Texas Highway 46, pass U.S. Highway 281, and continue on Texas Highway 46 for another 7 miles. Watch for signs to the park. It is best to make reservations well in advance for camping. Honey Creek State Natural Area is within the park boundaries and is a pleasant morning hike. To contact the park, call 210/438-2656.

In 1986 the Texas Legislature passed a bill creating the Water Oriented Recreation District (WORD) to manage the Guadalupe River Recreation Area, the most widely used recreation area in the state. The law provided for water safety, sanitation facilities, law enforcement, and a litter abatement program. WORD is funded by a user fee, so 15 cents on every tube rental and 75 cents on every raft and canoe rental goes to the district. The district provides waterproof trash bags to all the outfitters, who distribute them to people so that they can bring their trash back with them. Chemical toilets and trash barrels are now found every 2 miles along the river bank. River rangers patrol the river and assist in law enforcement and public safety education. The district passed an ordinance prohibiting glass and styrofoam, because glass is the worst river safety hazard and styrofoam has the biggest environmental impact on fish and wildlife. We commend Comal County and the Texas Legislature for the work they are doing to manage and protect the Guadalupe River.

Other rivers in the local area are the San Gabriel, Blanco, Pedernales, and Comal Rivers. When flowing, these rivers make good paddling, but be aware that water levels are frequently quite low and occasionally too high.

SAFETY TIPS

1. Wear a life jacket when in and on the water.

2. Limit use of alcohol.

3. Drink plenty of water.

4. Tube with another person; it is safer and more fun.

5. Walk around (portage) dangerous white water or any area you do not feel comfortable with.

6. Wear old tennis shoes to protect your feet.

7. Leave the river cleaner than you found it.

8. Do not take glass or styrofoam, as these are hazardous to you and the environment.

9. Avoid tube burn; cover your arms to the elbow.

10. Avoid sunburn with sunscreen and protective clothing.

11. Anchor eyeglasses with a string or special elastic guard.

12. Do not tie tubes together.

ORGANIZATIONS

Austin Paddling Club   835-1447

Austin Sierra Club   860-2993

University of Texas Recreational Sports   471-1093
(for classes in canoeing and kayaking)

REI (for activities on Barton Creek)   474-2393

Wilderness Supply (for activities on all Texas rivers)   476-3712

PUBLICATIONS

Kirkley, Gene. *A Guide to Texas Rivers and Streams*. Houston, Texas: Gulf Publishing, Lone Star Books, 1983.

McLeod, Gerald and Tom Grisham. *Barton Creek Guide*. Austin, Texas: *Austin Chronicle*, 1992.

Narramore, Bob, and Ben Nolen. *Rivers and Rapids* (formerly titled *Texas Rivers and Rapids*). Garland, Texas: Rivers and Rapids, 1992. This useful guide book, which covers mostly Texas rivers but also some rivers in Arkansas and Oklahoma, is available at most outfitting stores, or call 214-2-PADDLE.

OUTFITTERS

Colorado River outfitters:
Austin Canoe and Kayak   512/719-4386
Camp Chautauqua   512/264-1752
Colorado River Longhorn Canoe   409/732-3723
Zilker Canoe Rentals   512/478-3852

Guadalupe River outfitters:
Bezdek's Rentals   210/964-2244
Big Foot Canoe (Upper Guadalupe River)   210/885-7106
Gilligan's Island   210/964-2456
Gruene River Company   210/625-2800
Guadalupe Canoe Livery   210/885-4671
Guadalupe River Floats   210/964-3740
Guadalupe River Station   210/964-2850
Herb's Tube Rental   210/964-2450
Jerry's Rental   210/625-2036
K & L Ranch   210/625-3038
Lazy L & L Rental   210/964-3455
Little Ponderosa River Outfitters   210/964-3202
Maricopa Lodge Rentals   210/964-3600
Mountain Breeze   210/964-2484
(O)aces Cantina R Raft Company   210/620-7238
Rainbow Camp Rentals   210/964-2227

Rio Raft Company	210/964-3613
River Bank Outfitters	210/625-4928
River Road Camp Rentals	210/629-7325
River Road Rentals	210/964-2687
River Sports	210/964-2488
Rockin 'R' River Rides	210/629-6315
Roy's Rentals	210/964-3721
Shanty Tubes	210/964-3990
Texas Canoe Trails	210/907-3375
Tube Haus	210/964-2667
Whitewater Sports	210/964-3800

San Marcos River outfitters:

Pecan Park, Tom Goynes	512/392-6171
Spencer Canoes	512/357-6113
T G Canoe Rental	512/353-3946

Rowing

Thanks to some of the best rowing conditions in the world, Austin is gaining a reputation around the country as the best place to train year-round. Many college teams, such as the University of Minnesota and the University of Wisconsin, come to Austin over Christmas break to get some "water time."

Town Lake offers nearly 7 miles of undisturbed water from **Tom Miller Dam** to **Longhorn Dam**. The tree-lined shores offer protection from excessive wind, and a city ordinance ensures that the only power boats on the lake are coaching launches. Town Lake's course through the middle of Austin allows easy access to everyone living both north and south of the river.

Each year at least 3 major regattas are organized by the Austin Rowing Club. The Head of the Colorado is a 5,000-meter race against the clock, put on every fall. In March a 1,000-meter and 2,000-meter sprint race, known as the Heart of Texas Regatta, marks the start of spring racing. Finally, in August a short sprint is raced during the annual Aqua Festival. In 1991 Austin was the site of the Masters National Championship Regatta.

Rowers in Austin belong to one of 3 clubs and row out of one of 2 boathouses. Austin Rowing Club, situated on **Town Lake** just below the Four Seasons Hotel, caters to all types of rowers but concentrates on large team boats. Their facilities include a spacious boathouse, a weight and rowing ergometer room, and showers.

The University of Texas Crew Team is a competitive club sport. They row out of the Austin Rowing Club and compete in races from Boston to San Diego. In their short history, the team has produced several elite rowers and one National Team member.

Texas Rowing is a smaller club located a quarter of a mile east of MoPac on the hike-and-bike trail just south of the Austin High School football field. The club specializes in teaching people to row in singles and doubles and features private one-on-one instruction.

All 3 of these clubs welcome people who have never rowed before but want to learn.

ORGANIZATIONS

Austin Rowing Club	472-0700
Texas Rowing	482-8646
University of Texas Crew Team Division of Recreational Sports	471-1093

■ Sailing and Windsurfing

Sailing puts you in direct contact with the powers of nature—the wind, the water, and the sun. The thrill comes when you trim your sail to catch this power, for in an instant you start sailing as fast as the wind and sculpting a wake in the water. Sound like fun? Sure it is, but be cautious. Sailors must swim well and wear a personal flotation device approved by the Coast Guard.

How do you get started? If you are a student or an employee of the University of Texas, you may join the UT Sailing Club. The club has its own boats on **Lake Travis**, and club members give lessons. Sailing lessons are also available with:

■ U.S. Coast Guard Auxiliary

■ Bob Wentz Park at Windy Point (266-2544); take RM 620 and
turn north onto Comanche Trail.

While the Coast Guard Auxiliary does not provide a telephone
number that you can call to find out when lessons are scheduled, it
does post ads about its lessons in the newspaper about 3 or 4 weeks
in advance.

The Texas Sailing Academy, at Lakeway Marina on Lake Travis,
provides a state-accredited course in boating safety and sailing
instruction that ranges from basic sailing to bareboat charter
certification in boats 19' to 42' long. You have the option of private
lessons in your boat or group instruction in one of the boats in the
academy's fleet. TSA's instructors are licensed by the U.S. Coast
Guard as Masters and accredited by the state as boating safety
instructors. You may rent a sailboat by the half day, full day,

weekend, or week or charter a boat with or without a captain. Sailboats in TSA's fleet are mono-hull sloops ranging in size from 19' to 42' and can accommodate up to 12 people. Call 261-6193 or, better yet, visit TSA at the Lakeway Marina.

If you already sail or windsurf, you will find plenty of scenery along the Highland Lakes. One of the closest is Lake Travis just 30 minutes away. It has high bluffs and steep banks with many inlets and coves, but most sailing takes place on the main body of the lake. You can view the Austin Yacht Club's Sunday afternoon Regatta from the cliffs and hills. Take RM 2222 west to RM 620, the road that connects the north and south sides of Lake Travis. On the north side, continue on RM 2222, which becomes Bullock Hollow after you cross RM 620, and follow this road until it intersects with RM 2769, where you will see **Cypress Creek Park** on the left.

On the south side of the lake on RM 620 about a mile west of Mansfield Dam, Hudson Bend Road to the right will take you to the Austin Yacht Club, a club for seasoned sailors. Follow Hudson Bend Road for about a mile, then turn right onto Beacon Drive and follow Beacon Drive about a mile to the club.

A couple of miles farther west on RM 620 you can turn right onto Clara Van Trail and drive a mile to find Hurst Harbor Marina. Or go a little farther along RM 620 and turn right instead onto Lakeway Boulevard to reach Lakeway Marina. Alternatively, Texas Highway 71 going west will take you through Bee Caves to access the lake from the south.

If you don't have a sailboat, a number of places will rent one to you, including Club Nautico at Hurst Harbor Marina (266-2922) and Commander's Point Yacht Basin (266-2333), a quarter mile west of Mansfield Dam down Commander's Point Drive. Boats there range from 23' to 30'. Boats can also be rented at Bob Wentz Park at Windy Point (266-2544) and the privately owned Windy Point Park (250-1963), located close together. Take RM 2222, turn left onto RM 620, go about a mile, turn right onto Comanche Trail, and drive about 3 miles, passing Hippie Hollow Park. If you own a sailboat, several marinas rent slips or dry storage as well.

Good places to launch your boat include Mansfield Dam Park off RM 620, Cypress Creek Park on the corner of Bullock Hollow and RM 2769, or any of the municipal, state, or LCRA parks. Another good launch is Sandy Creek Park on Lime Creek Road. From RM 620 follow RM 2769 through Volente to Lime Creek Road or take RM 1431 west to approach it from the north.

Windsurfers enjoy the optimum wind conditions generated off low-lying terrain. Popular areas on Lake Travis are Windy Point and Lakeway. Other good choices include Inks Lake, off Texas Highway 21 near Burnet, and Lake Georgetown, about 25 miles north of Austin. Take IH 35 north to Georgetown, turn left onto RM 2338, and follow the signs to Cedar Brakes, Jim Hogg, or Russell Parks. Lake Georgetown as well as Lake Granger are on the San Gabriel River. To find Lake Granger, go north to Georgetown, turn right onto FM 971, and go about 15 miles to Granger. Cross Texas Highway 95 to locate the north entrance to the lake.

About 65 miles east of Austin, one can sail Lake Somerville. Take U.S. Highway 290 to Giddings and then turn north onto FM 180 to the entrance on Yegua Creek.

Better known to Austinites is Canyon Lake, 65 miles south of Austin past San Marcos. Take IH 35 south, turn west on FM 306, and follow the signs to this lake.

If you are willing to venture even farther out, head for Lake Buchanan, the largest of the Highland Lakes. This immense lake offers the most variety, from sandy beaches and mud flats to limestone bluffs and waterfalls.

■ Snorkeling and Scuba Diving

Skin diving is quite popular in Central Texas, and the silent underwater world attracts more and more visitors each year. It is a world of fish and other aquatic life; of flowing vegetation, caves and rock formations; of sunken boats and even treasure—if only in recovered watches or diving and fishing gear. Skin diving is divided into 2 categories: snorkeling (also called free diving) and scuba (acronym for *self-contained underwater breathing apparatus*). The most important thing to remember in both types of diving is the buddy system. *Never dive alone!* Always have someone with you and keep track of each other at all times. When snorkeling with a buddy, swim "one-up and one-down" so the person on the surface can keep an eye on the person underwater and assist if a problem occurs.

In the 1930s and 1940s prior to World War II, skin diving became popular in the United States. Early equipment was crude, with a section of garden hose used for the snorkel. In the summer of 1943 in France, Jacques-Yves Cousteau and his team used a new device called the Aqua-lung to make more than 500 dives in the Marne River. Not an overnight success, scuba diving was limited during the 1950s and 1960s. With safer and more comfortable equipment in the 1980s, it became accessible to the general public. Anyone in reasonably good physical condition with some swimming ability can learn to dive, although children must be at least 12 years old to get scuba certification.

SNORKELING

The snorkeler uses a mask, fins, snorkel, and optional flotation vest. You can purchase basic snorkeling equipment at any dive shop and most reputable sporting goods stores, but avoid the toy stores. Cheap "toy" masks with plastic lenses fog badly, usually leak, and scratch if you look at them hard. Snorkels with "automatic valves" are nothing more than a ping-pong ball in a cage at the intake end of the snorkel; they should not be depended on because they always leak. Stay away especially from masks with built-in snorkels, which are very unsafe! Diving is "equipment intensive," and most of the risks inherent to the sport can be avoided with the proper use of good-quality equipment and training. Snorkeling lessons are given by the Austin Nature Center (327-8181) for preschool children through adults, and any one of the local dive shops will be happy to help you select equipment and instruct you on its use and care. Pick a dive shop that will let you try out the fit of the equipment in their pool before you purchase anything.

In snorkeling, you depend on the surface for air, usually cruising facedown on the surface while watching the underwater panorama beneath you. While limited by the amount of time that you can hold your breath, you can even dive down to explore the underwater world. **Barton Springs** and the **San Marcos River** offer a great variety of fish to see, and both can be snorkeled in the winter because water temperatures remain relatively constant year-round.

In fact, the San Marcos River is reputed to be one of the best snorkeling locations in the state. Maximum depth is about 15 feet, and a year-round temperature of 72°F makes for particularly good winter diving when the summer crowds of swimmers and tubers are absent. Visibility is usually very good, especially in winter and early spring. Entry points are **City Park**, **Rio Vista Park**, and below the IH 35 bridge. The main disadvantage here is the swift current, but pockets can be found where leisurely diving may be enjoyed.

Like the San Marcos, the **Comal River** in New Braunfels is best in winter and early spring when its waters are not clouded by the crowds. Maximum depth is about 20 feet just above the dam, and the year-round temperature is a comfortable 75°F. This spot is also popular with scuba divers. Again, there is a fairly strong current to contend with. When diving in the deep area above the dam, take care not to get swept over it, or through the "tubers' chute", which can be a pretty bumpy ride. Entry points are just below **Landa Park** (across from the golf course), starting about 100 yards upstream from the railroad bridge, all the way down to the dam. Much of this, however, is shallow, trashed out, and not very inspiring.

Another area is Hamilton Pool but it can be crowded in the summer. Lake Travis parks offer good snorkeling, too, but the lake water is not as clear and the surface is rougher than the rivers, especially on weekends with the boat wakes. Visibility in **Lake Travis** and **Canyon Lake**, the 2 most popular, can range from 0 to 30 feet under ideal conditions.

SCUBA DIVING

Scuba diving is much more complex than snorkeling. Divers carry their own air supply, thus cutting them free from the surface. Certification is required before purchasing or renting equipment. A certification class entails about 6 classroom and pool sessions with 5 open water dives in such a body of water as Lake Travis. After this "open water certification," many divers go on to get advanced and special certification in underwater photography, underwater navigation, night diving, and many other specialties. Scuba diving certification does not expire, but area dive stores give refresher classes for those who dive only on vacation and need to update their skills. Certification classes and equipment are available in the Austin area at:

- Aquatic Adventures   219-1220
  12129 RM 620N #440

- Double D Diving   331-2199
  8644 Spicewood Springs Road

- Pisces Scuba   258-6646
  11401 RM 2222

- Scubaland Adventures   339-0733
  9515 N. Lamar

- See Sea Divers   258-8000
  13376 Research Boulevard

- Tom's Dive and Ski   451-3425
  5909 Burnet Road

Classes are also taught through UT Recreational Sports and other
organizations. Check "Divers" under the Yellow Pages for new
businesses. All area stores sponsor local dive trips.

For both scuba diving and snorkeling in the San Marcos River, a
good resource is The Dive Shop (512/396-3483) at 1911 RM 12, San
Marcos, Texas, 78666. Don Dibble, who runs this store, is highly
respected by local divers. The shop's open water certification course,
spread over 3 weeks, offers 24 hours of instruction and 5 snorkel
dives in Canyon Lake. Students must have their own mask, fins,
and snorkel. More advanced classes are offered, too, such as an
underwater photography course that is half lecture and half water
instruction.

Lake Travis is known as one of the best places to dive in Texas.
People come from all over the state for the open water certification
in this lake. Some good places for diving along the lake include
Mansfield Dam Recreation Area and **Hippie Hollow Park.**
(See Chapter 2, *At the Park*, for more information).

Windy Point Park (266-9459), a privately owned park on Lake
Travis, is rated as one of the best diving and training sites for
beginners and experts alike. Four wooden staircases with hand
rails make entries and exits easy, and the terraced limestone
bottom drops quickly to nearly 200 feet as you swim out from shore.

At the bottom divers find boat wrecks plus unique metal sculptures of angel fish, a sea turtle, a diver, a shark, and a manatee put there by the owner, who has dived himself for over 20 years. Take RM 2222 west, turn left onto RM 620, go approximately a mile to a flashing yellow light, and turn right onto Comanche Trail. Go 3 miles, passing the Oasis Restaurant, Hippie Hollow, and Bob Wentz Park at Windy Point, then turn left onto Windy Point Road and look for the entrance to the park immediately to the right.

Area dive stores also sponsor trips farther out to such places as the Gulf Coast, which features the Flower Gardens, oil rigs, and sunken shipwrecks. More exotic trips are also organized to Florida, the Bahamas, Cayman Islands and Mexico. Most stores put out a newsletter with details of forthcoming trips to these wonderful faraway places.

Up
IN THE
Air
5

■ Hang Gliding and Paragliding

In hang gliding the flier is as free as a bird. Depending on your skill and experience, you can simply coast to the bottom of a hill or take off and ride the thermals and ridge drafts (air currents deflected upwards by hills and ridges) for hours. Lift is gained from a large flying wing, variously called a hang glider, glider, or ultra-light aircraft. The pilot is suspended in a harness below the glider. There are no regular controls and no cockpit. The craft is maneuvered by shifting one's weight or warping the surface of the glider.

As long as you weigh at least 70 pounds, you can hang glide. Hang gliding is not an overly strenuous sport, but you should be in reasonably good physical shape. The gliders, which weigh about 50 pounds, are not easy to handle on the ground. Hang gliders usually launch on foot from the top of a hill or cliff and are also towed on land. The price for a used glider starts at $1,000; a new one starts at $2,000.

In tandem flying, an instructor can be up with you to take over in an emergency. Most accidents in this sport result from pilot error, so it is important to start with competent instruction and progress slowly and carefully. The United States Hang Gliding Association regulates the sport by issuing licenses and proficiency levels (I to IV) to its members. Certain levels are required to launch from many difficult sites. At present there is no governmental regulation or licensing.

Jeff Hunt of Red River Air Craft (467-2529) and Steve Burns of Austin Air Sports (474-1669) both offer instruction in hang gliding. Instruction costs from $69 to $599 depending upon the level you wish to achieve. Accommodations can be made for those in wheelchairs on tandem flights.

Murchison Junior High School in Austin, **Lake Travis**, and **Windemere Air Park** off Texas Highway 71 are some of the sites used for hang gliding. Another popular site is **Pack Saddle Mountain**, about an hour and a half from Austin on the way to Llano. Take Texas Highway 71 going west. About 17 miles before you reach Llano you will see a historical marker about Pack Saddle Mountain on your right, next to County Road 309. Turn right onto the road and go for about 1.5 miles until you see the launch ramp at the end of the mountain. A group should be there most weekends when the wind is blowing from the south.

Paragliding is a sister sport to hang gliding. Both types of gliders are launched by foot. The main difference between the two is that the hang glider has a rigid wing with aluminum supports while the paraglider has a flexible, self-inflating wing with no rigid, internal supports. For that reason the paraglider is lighter, even though the canopy is larger. It weighs only 23 pounds and can be packed in a backpack. The paraglider also travels more slowly at 3 to 25 miles an hour as opposed to 20 to 70 miles an hour for the hang glider. The sites for paragliding in the Austin area are the same as those for hang gliding.

The United States Hang Gliding Association regulates paragliding in addition to hang gliding. Those wishing to become a pilot will spend between $600 and $1,200 for instruction, which is offered by Hill Country Paragliding (contact Marie Osowski at 794-1160 or 800/664-1160). Austin Air Sports (474-1669) offers instruction in paragliding and ultralight flying in addition to hang gliding. A new canopy runs from $800 to $3,800, and the backup ballistic reserve is about $800 to $1,000. Equipment is also available for rent.

■ Soaring

While the term "soaring" is often applied to both sailplaning and hang gliding, what it actually means is the use of rising warm-air currents, or thermals, to gain altitude and remain in unpowered flight for long periods of time. While it is possible for skillful hang gliders, soaring is much easier and more natural in sailplanes, and the term is more generally applied to that sport. Sailplane soaring is considered by its advocates to be the safest of the aerial sports. The minimum age to solo is only 14 and the minimum age to hold a pilot's license is 16.

In the hands of an experienced pilot, it is possible to keep a plane aloft all day and cover hundreds of miles. Soaring may be a strange sensation to one who is used to powered flight. Noise and vibration are conspicuously absent, and the only sound is the rush of the wind. The cockpit is small. Even a 2-seat trainer has the second seat behind the first, and the legs are extended out in front as if seated on a very low pillow. But the bubble canopy gives a feeling of being out in the wide open spaces.

A soaring club operates out of the **Fault Line Flyers Glider Port** just west of Briggs, and some members are usually active there every nice weekend. The first Saturday of every month starting at noon is a demonstration day where visitors can take a 20-30-minute ride in a tandem sailplane. Children and those in wheelchairs may go on the demonstration flights. The Glider Port is midway between Austin and Lampasas. Take U.S. Highway 183 north to Briggs and turn left onto County Road 210. Two miles down on your left is the Glider Port. While there is no sign, you can't miss all the sailplanes in the field.

Membership in the Fault Line Flyers is open to anyone who wishes to buy a share in the organization and pay monthly dues. The share may be sold to other individuals or to the club. The club owns 4 sailplanes, a tow plane, a tow car, and a winch (a winch reels in cable for towing). There are fees for air tows or car tows. Everyone who is active or flies is expected to do a fair share of the maintenance and other work. For new members who are not licensed, the club has several instructors, who donate their nominal fees to the club. You can get fully trained and licensed through any of them. For further information, contact Floyd Bates at 263-2233.

The **Boerne Stage Airfield** in Boerne also offers accommodations, sailplanes, and instruction. Call Bob Bruce at 210/981-2345 for more information. To get to the airfield, go south on IH 35 to San Antonio, take the Loop 410W Exit, and get on I 10 West going to El Paso. After about 10 minutes, take the Boerne Stage Road Exit at Leon Springs. Turn left onto the road, go 3 miles to a 4-way stop sign, and then turn right. The entrance is on the right after about 2.5 miles.

■ Hot Air Ballooning

The sight of a large, brightly-colored hot air balloon floating over the city or countryside can be truly poetic. Hot air ballooning, which started in 1783, is the oldest and most natural means for human flight. Its fans also claim that it is the safest. The best time for ballooning is early in the morning at sunrise because the wind is calm and cool. The greater the temperature difference inside and outside the balloon, the greater the lift and the smaller the heat requirement.

Heat is supplied by a high-efficiency propane burner attached above the gondola (basket), which heats the air in the envelope (balloon) through its open bottom. Since warm air rises, this creates the lift that flies the balloon (made of flame-resistant ripstop nylon). The direction of flight is totally dependent on the prevailing winds, but altitude can be controlled by turning on the burner to rise or venting hot air out of the envelope to descend. When the burner is off, the flight is absolutely silent, and since the balloon drifts with the air mass, there is no sense of motion. Pilots describe it as a beautiful but eerie sensation.

Ballooning is controlled by the Federal Aviation Administration, which licenses pilots. The Balloon Federation of America, a

national organization, promotes the sport and sanctions meets and competitions.

The Central Texas Ballooning Association (479-9421) offers monthly competitions, weather permitting, and an annual Balloon "Moonglow" at **Zilker Park** in December. This association meets the second Monday of each month at 7:30 p.m. at Tres Amigos (at U.S. Highway 290 and U.S. Highway 183), and visitors are welcome. Several local companies offer flight instruction or specialty flights. Among them are Air Wolf Adventures (836-2305), Austin Aeronauts Hot Air Balloons (440-1492 or 800/444-3257), and Balloon Port of Austin (835-6058). Prices are $150 or more for 1 person for a one-hour flight. Austin Aeronauts Hot Air Balloons offers a specialty flight over **Lake Travis** at sunrise, a night flight from **Zilker Park** over the city before sunrise, and a flight over **Enchanted Rock**. Austin Aeronauts has a sling available, which is attached to the side of the basket, to accommodate those in wheelchairs.

Lessons are $150-$300 per hour. Used balloons begin at $5,000 and new balloons are from $10,000 on up. A private license requires 10 hours of flight time with the instructor plus written and oral tests and a check ride.

■ Skydiving

Basically, the term "skydiving" refers purely to sport parachuting and ranges all the way from the beginner's tandem dive to long free-falls with groups of jumpers falling in formation and landing accurately on a predetermined target. The advanced free-fall is about as close as one can get to the sensation of flying, Superman-style. While it appears to be dangerous, the sport is really quite safe when done with proper instruction and supervision. The main chute (canopy) is always backed up by a reserve chute and the chance of both malfunctioning is very remote indeed.

Skydiving is regulated by the United States Parachute Association (USPA), which issues licenses, approves drop zones, and sets standards for the sport. No matter how advanced the jumper, the reserve chute must always be packed by a USPA-licensed rigger. This further increases the margin of safety.

The University of Texas Union Informal Classes (471-0270) offers an introduction to skydiving. UT offers the class most Saturdays during the school semester. It includes only 1 tandem jump, and further activity must be continued through Skydive San Marcos (800/726-9267 or 512/488-2214), whose instructors and facilities are those used by UT. All equipment is furnished, and there is an extensive prejump briefing on the day of the jump. Facilities are at **Fentress Air Park**, about 45 minutes from downtown Austin. Go south on IH 35 to Texas Highway 80, then go southeast on Texas Highway 80 for 12.8 miles to the airfield.

Another USPA-affiliated drop zone is **Temple Municipal Airport**. Contact Skydive Temple at 817/778-4200 for more information.

OUT WITH FAUNA AND FRIENDS 6

▌Birdwatching

Birding in Austin is special and unique, keeping longtime residents entertained with year-round variety and affording excellent opportunities for checklisters to add to North American life records. The city lies on the line considered to divide eastern from western North America, and the ranges of many eastern and western species overlap in Austin. A number of Mexican and Central American species reach the northern limits of their distributions in Central Texas, while the area marks the southern terminus of the winter migration for many northern species. Finally, because Austin is located on the central North American migration flyway, almost the entire year is migration time.

Begin your survey of Austin birds at the city's center—the **State Capitol**. The wooded lawns have long provided shelter and feeding grounds for migrant songbirds, and regular noontime birding sessions are hosted by local birders during April and early May. Year-round residents include Red-bellied Woodpeckers, the ever-present Great-tailed Grackles, Tufted Titmice, Chickadees, and Cardinals. At night, Screech Owls and Great Horned Owls are common, while in summer Common Nighthawks are drawn to insects attracted by the bright lights illuminating the Capitol dome.

All city parks offer excellent birding opportunities. Stately live oaks, cedar elms, and pecan trees provide leafy refuges and feeding opportunities for spring migrants. During March, April, and early May the trees are full of warblers, vireos, and tanagers fueling up for the next leg of their journey northward. Almost any of the species that cross the Gulf or migrate through Central America may appear at this time. The most profitable birding areas other than the Capitol are **Waterloo Park**, **Northwest Park**, the **Barton Creek Greenbelt, the hike-and-bike trails along Town Lake**, and any of the other numerous streams. Be sure and see the Monk Parakeets nesting on lightpoles at the athletic fields in **Zilker Park** and listen for the bubbly cheer of a Carolina Wren along the Town Lake Trail.

East of town the sewage treatment plant at **Hornsby Bend** hosts rare and unique species almost any time of the year. Wintering and migrating waterfowl may include any of the North American ducks, while Black-bellied Whistling Ducks are resident during the summer. In the fall of 1992, a Surf Scoter and a Red-necked Phalarope were on the ponds at the same time. The ponds have hosted migrating Whooping Cranes and Hudsonian Godwits, while Osprey and Peregrine Falcons are becoming regular visitors. In the prairies, woodlands, and riverbanks abutting the plant may be found almost any bird that ever appears in Austin.

Several state parks within a one-hour drive of Austin sample the different types of habitat found in the area. Central Texas is home to 2 endangered bird species, the Golden-cheeked Warbler and the Black-capped Vireo. Both nest in spring and summer in the Hill Country within and west of the city limits. A major Hill Country bioreserve is being assembled to protect these and other endangered plant and animal species.

McKinney Falls State Park, at the southeastern city limits, hosts Great Horned, Barred, Barn, and Screech Owls; Great and Snowy Egrets; and Killdeer and Belted Kingfishers year-round. Ringed and Green Kingfishers have been sighted during summer months. Greenbacked and Little Blue Herons are common at the confluence of **Williamson** and **Onion Creeks**, and Painted Buntings nest through the summer. Listen for the singing males atop brushy trees and shrubs.

East of Austin along Texas Highway 71, **Bastrop** and **Buescher**

State Parks are within a one-hour drive of Austin and are linked by a park road. Watch for Crested Caracaras wheeling in the air over woods and pastures between Austin and Bastrop. In **Bastrop State Park** look for the Pine Warblers, which are resident year-round in the isolated stand of loblolly pines, the westernmost extension of the ranges of both pine and warbler species. Along the park road, the flora gradually change from pine to eastern hardwood forests typical of riparian bottomlands. A small resident population of Pileated Woodpeckers can be seen occasionally at utility cuts that cross the road. During winter **Buescher State Park** hosts large numbers of small birds from the north. Look for Brown Creepers, Ruby- and Golden-crowned Kinglets, and Yellow-rumped Warblers. Robins, Cedar Waxwings, and American Goldfinches may be found from January through early spring.

South of Luling off U.S. Highway 183 on the San Marcos River, **Palmetto State Park** is widely regarded as the area's birding hot spot, especially during spring migration. An aquifer flowing from a geologic uplift just to the west feeds the artesian spring, which in turn nourishes an isolated palmetto swamp. Northern Parulas and Red-shouldered Hawks nest in the park, as do Red-headed, Downy, Hairy, and rarely-seen Pileated Woodpeckers as well as Eastern, Western and Great-crested Flycatchers. Almost any of the eastern warblers, vireos, and flycatchers may be seen during migration, and several are summer residents. Watch for buntings, orioles, and grossbeaks as well.

About 40 miles west of the city, **Pedernales Falls State Park** exemplifies Hill Country habitat. In the steep canyons cut through cedar- and oak-clad limestone hills, swimmers and tubers are accompanied by the brash, cascading call of the Canyon Wren. Black-crested Titmice, Golden-fronted Woodpeckers, and Scrub Jays take the place of their eastern counterparts. The park is an important, undisturbed breeding area for Golden-cheeked Warblers and Black-capped Vireos.

A slow drive along one of the many ranch roads in the Austin area may yield elegant Scissor-tailed Flycatchers, Eastern and Western Kingbirds, Eastern Meadowlarks, and several swallow species adorning fences and wires in summer. In winter, American Kestrels and Loggerhead Shrikes dominate the exposed perches, while during migrations Broad-winged and Swainson's Hawks are common. In winter, Northern Harriers hunt low over fields and pasᴗᴜres, and both Ferruginous and Rough-legged Hawks are seen with fair regularity. East of town and visible from FM 969, an egret and heron rookery hosts Cattle, Common, and Snowy Egrets as well as Little Blue and Tri-colored Herons.

This overview just barely scratches the surface of birding possibilities in and around Austin. Almost any North American species may turn up here, and even experienced Austin birders are frequently able to add to their life lists without leaving town. The Travis Audubon Society has a detailed checklist for birds in the Austin area and a **Birding Hotline** (483-0952) that reports current and unusual bird sightings and gives information about their organization's meetings and field trips. Most Texas state parks have checklists on birds seen in the parks. Four excellent books are listed below. They extensively cover birds seen in the Austin area and include checklists, maps, and advice on where and when to see them. Good birding!

PUBLICATIONS

Kutac, Edward A. *Birder's Guide to Texas*. Houston, Texas: Gulf Publishing, 1989.

Kutac, Edward A., and S. Christopher Caran. *Birds and Wildlife of Central Texas*. Austin, Texas: University of Texas Press, 1994.

Rappole, John H., Gene W. Blacklock. *Birds of Texas: A Field Guide*. College Station, Texas: Texas A&M University Press, 1994.

Tveten, John L. *Birds of Texas*. Fredericksburg, Texas: Shearer Publishing, 1993.

■ Dog Walks

Popular areas to walk dogs are the greenbelts and hike-and-bike trails described in detail in Chapters 1 and 2. For the safety of both people and animals, dogs must be on leashes while walking these trails (a short leash is recommended). A city ordinance specifies 11 areas, listed below, where dogs may run unleashed "provided that such dogs, while in the designated areas, shall remain under the *immediate personal supervision and command of their owner or handler.*" In other words, owners should be prepared to control their dogs if necessary. Don't forget your "pooper scooper."

- Auditorium Shores: the stretch from South 1st Street west to Bouldin Creek, before you get to Lamar

- Zilker Park: that portion of the park bounded by Barton Springs Road, Lou Neff Drive, and Stratford Drive

- Far West Boulevard: the right-of-way located between Great Northern Boulevard and Shoal Creek Boulevard

- Robert Mueller Municipal Airport: that portion bounded by Old Manor Road, Manor Road, the airport fence, and Lovell Drive

- Red Bud Isle

- Onion Creek District Park: that portion south of Chunn Road

- Northeast District Park: that portion bounded by Decker Lake Road, Crystal Brook Drive, and the Missouri-Kansas-Texas railroad right-of-way

- Walnut Creek Metropolitan Park: that portion bounded by Cedar Bend Drive, Walnut Creek, and the park fences on the east and west sides

- Lake Austin Metropolitan Park: that portion bounded by City Park Drive, the park fence on the west side, Turkey Creek, and the top ridge of the bluff line overlooking Lake Austin

- Shoal Creek Hike-and-Bike Trail: the stretch from 24th Street to 29th Street

- Northwood Estates: a 3-acre park at the northwest corner of IH 35 and Riverside Drive

While the first 10 areas have been listed in the city ordinance as being leash-free zones, Northwood Estates was just added to the list in late 1994.

Dogs participate in the pet parade held in August every year in
conjunction with Aqua Festival, and they perform feats that will
delight and amaze you at dog frisbee events held at **Zilker Park**.
For a calendar of events contact the Visitor Information Center
(478-0098 or 800/888-8AUS) at 201 East 2nd Street, Austin, Texas,
78701. Other locations where visitor information is provided are the
State Capitol (General Land Office at the southeast corner of the
Capitol grounds) and **Robert Mueller Municipal Airport**. The
Austin Parks and Recreation Department may also know when
these events are scheduled.

■ Horseback Riding

Horses figure prominently in the history of Texas, and Texans still
enjoy them. Many fine stables and organizations in the Austin area
offer riding lessons and opportunities for the young and old. You

can choose among carriage rides, English or Western lessons and riding competitions, trail rides, parade rides, children's riding camps, and birthday-party pony rides. For a fee you can have a campfire supper complete with cowboys to lead fireside singing or stage an old-fashioned, wild-Western holdup or other high-spirited entertainment, complete with horses.

Visitors may enjoy a carriage ride around downtown Austin and the Capitol. From the front of the **Capitol** tours run from 10 a.m. to 4 p.m. Saturdays and Sundays. From the Hyatt Regency Hotel, tours of **Town Lake** lasting 20 minutes run from dusk to 11 p.m. on Fridays and Saturdays. From the Driskill Hotel a tour of Town Lake lasts 80 minutes. Tours of **Sixth Street** originate from the Radisson Hotel and from the Four Seasons Hotel. Midnight rides are available on 6th and Trinity Streets. Like taxis, the carriages can pick you up and drop you off from a variety of downtown locations; ask the driver for prices. Reservations are not required, but to guarantee a carriage at your convenience, contact **Austin Carriage Services** at 243-0044 or 8413 South FM 973, Austin, Texas, 78719.

Although developed parks are often too small and crowded for horses, one city park with an equestrian trail is **Mary Moore Searight Metropolitan Park** at 907 Slaughter Lane. Two Travis County parks that allow horseback riding are **Webberville Park** in Webberville, off FM 969, and **Pace Bend Park** along Lake Travis near Briarcliff off RM 2322. Designated areas are marked; no reservations are needed. The Lower Colorado River Authority maintains primitive recreational areas (Resource Areas) along the Highland Lakes which are also suitable for riding. **Turkey Bend East Resource Area**, with 400 acres, has parking space for horse trailers. **Narrows Resource Area**, with 250 acres, is unimproved but offers plenty of room for horses. **Gloster Bend Park** and **Cedar Point Park** are other possibilities, but they are smaller so check them out before you haul a horse, as they may not suit your needs. For maps and information, call LCRA (473-4083 or 800/776-5272 ext. 4083). You may also address inquiries to LCRA as follows:

Lower Colorado River Authority
Land Resources Division
P. O. Box 220
Austin, Texas 78767

The state park system includes a number of parks with riding trails. Near Austin are **Pedernales Falls State Park, Lake Somerville State Park,** and the **Hill Country State Natural Area,** all within 100 miles of Austin. For more information, contact the Texas Department of Parks and Wildlife (389-4890) at 4200 Smith School Road, Austin, Texas, 78744.

The University of Texas Outdoor Recreation Program (471-1093), at Gregory Gym Room 31, offers hour-long trail rides about twice monthly through local stables. Rates are $21 per hour for UT people and $24 per hour for the public. About twice annually, this group enjoys extended trail rides through breathtaking scenery in Big Bend National Park (novices included) or Mexico (experienced riders only). A memorable adventure! Each trip lasts about 5 days, and rates are about $350 for UT students or closer to $400 for others. This includes transportation, guides, and food on the trail.

Travis County 4-H Clubs offer an excellent program for horse lovers of all ages. Under the leadership of Jean Koenig (478-2201) and County Extension Agent Jim Smith, youngsters can participate in a number of horse shows, clinics, trail rides, and other horse-related activities. Those over 18 can participate in 2 annual horse shows. Participants are taught English pleasure riding and Western pleasure and trail riding. All shows are held at the Texas Heritage Center, and show rules are similar to those of official quarter-horse shows. The show entry fee is $5. Skilled instructors, some nationally ranked, teach the fine points of horsemanship at several clinics held annually. Local veterinarians also hold clinics on horse care and health. Many clinics are free; a charge of $5 defrays the expenses of others.

The Austin Founder's Trail Ride, held annually in March, is an extended trail ride covering different routes each year. A typical trail begins at New Braunfels, proceeds on by Satler, ', the Blue Hole at Wimberley, Kyle, and Creedmoor, ending with a parade down Congress Avenue in Austin. Novices may choose from "a good string of rental horses." People with disabilities may join the trail ride by special arrangement, accompanied by their own assistants, as required by individual needs. For more information, call Jean Mueller (477-4711).

Austin-area stables and equestrian centers offer a wide spectrum of riding experiences. In general a stable has a barn with stalls for the horses, feed and equipment storage, an exercise area, and an arena for lessons. Some may have only the barn and fenced land; others, multiple pens, indoor and outdoor arenas, bleachers, a clubhouse, an office, and extensive acreage for cross-country riding. The term *equestrian center* implies a larger, multi activity facility. Whatever the style, always call in advance to reserve a horse.

Because insurance for renting horses to the general public has become prohibitively expensive, skilled instructors evaluate the ability of riders. In general, novice riders take riding lessons instead of renting horses. When the instructor is satisfied with the level of ability, the rider may proceed along the trails. Novice and intermediate riders are accompanied on the trail by the instructor or guide. Only when the instructor becomes confident of the rider's ability may the rider venture off without the guide and then only if the insurance policy permits.

Typically, riders begin with lessons on rented horses. Lessons are available in English-or Western-style riding, dressage (training of the horse), jumping, riding cross-country over varied terrain, and even horse psychology. You may often lease a favorite mount. Individuals can usually arrange to join a group to take advantage of group rental rates. For those who own their own horses, stables provide lessons, boarding, grooming, exercise, veterinary care, and other convenient services for owner and horse. While some owners prefer to ride through the countryside, enjoying the scenery and fresh air, others seriously pursue excellence in horsemanship.

Though many stables remain private, serving only those who board horses there, the following stables offer services to the general public.

Bald Eagle Ranch (243-1340) in the Creedmoor area south of Austin beckons the rider and horse with 30 acres of open rolling grasslands. Complete with a lighted outdoor arena, the ranch offers not only lessons but also horse training and birthday-party pony rides. Need a fund-raiser? Consider a group trail ride organized through Bald Eagle Ranch. The address for the ranch is Route 1, Box 192A, Kyle, Texas, 78640. Drive south on IH 35, exit at FM 1327, go east 5 miles, then turn right onto FM 1625, and go straight 1.5 miles, ignoring a fork in the road. You will come to a T-intersection, where you turn left and proceed along a wide curve followed by a straight length of road. About 1.5 miles from the T-intersection, you come to a stop sign where you turn left again and proceed about a quarter of a mile. Bald Eagle Ranch is on the left. Look for the red barn and turn in the drive. There is no sign.

Bear Creek Stables (282-0250) has 20 acres and plans to expand to 100 acres in the scenic Hill Country along Bear Creek, where a trail by the creek is wooded and shady. Plenty of open space surrounds the large, lighted indoor and outdoor arenas. There are lessons in English-or Western-style riding, charged by the hour. Jumps, horse shows, guided trail rides, and a summer camp are other activities. A first-time rider should be at least 7 years old. Take Manchaca Road south to the T-intersection with FM 1626 and proceed west (right) on FM 1626 for 3 miles. Pass the Volunteer Fire Department and a sign on the right to "Townsley Cemetery." Take the next left turn at the Bear Creek subdivision sign, meander along to Bob Johnson Road, turn right and follow Bob Johnson Road almost to the end. Turn left at the Bear Creek Stables sign and follow the drive past the old Victorian house and the modern home, down the hill to the stables. The address is 13017 Bob Johnson Road, Manchaca, Texas, 78652.

Look for **Blue Star Riding Center** (243-2583) on U.S. Highway 183 south of FM 812. Here fresh breezes ripple through a wide sweep of prairie grasses under the blue Texas sky. On these 50 acres you will find room for cross-country riding as well as the usual English-or Western-style riding lessons, shows, and competitions. Charges by the hour. Barn parties with games on horseback, trail rides, riding clinics, and summer camp round out a full schedule of activities. A handsome thoroughbred stallion is at stud. Facilities include lighted indoor and outdoor arenas, a barn, pens, gear lockers, and a trailer for hauling horses to shows. Take U.S. Highway 183 south, pass FM 812, and go about 3.5 more miles. On the east side of the highway, look for the sign on the big blue barn. The exact address is 9513 S. Highway 183, Austin, Texas, 78747.

Bastrop Farms (303-0378) northeast of **Bastrop State Park**, is great for a ride in the pines. They offer riding lessons, trail rides, training, breeding, and boarding of horses. Small groups and individuals are escorted through the pine forests on Arabian and Saddlebred show horses. On-site rides are charged by the hour. Rides to area lakes, parks, and ranches are also offered; costs per hour vary. Trail rides are planned all year throughout Central Texas and also Canyon de Chelly and Monument Valley in Arizona. You can bring your own horse on any of their rides. Take Texas

Highway 71 east to Bastrop, turn north on Texas Highway 21, turn left on County Road 133 (just after divided highway ends), Bastrop Farms is the first gate on the right. The address is Route 1, 1390 Cardinal Drive, Paige, Texas, 78659.

Ol' Cactus Jack's dude ranch (263-2388) is west of Oak Hill on Texas Highway 71 an eighth of a mile past RM 620. It's just plain country, where dudes can ride over 300 scenic Hill Country acres along Little Barton Creek. The restrooms are portables, but there is fun to be had here: day or moonlight trail rides, hayrides in October, a pavilion for barbecue, volleyball, horseshoes, campfires, and sing-alongs. This is a good place for parties, reunions, or just a moonlight trail ride or Halloween Hayride with your sweetie. Open 9 a.m. to 7 p.m. every day except Sunday, when the hours are 10 a.m. to 6 p.m. and Tuesday, when the ranch is closed. Address: 13433 West Highway 71, Austin, Texas, 78738.

The **Cameron Equestrian Center** (272-4301) in northeast Austin is a newly constructed facility with barns, pens, a large indoor arena, an outdoor arena, and a comfortable clubhouse/office on 60 acres. Besides boarding and training horses, the center provides lessons in English-and Western-style riding, vaulting and jumping, and gymnastic riding. The cost of a lesson varies with the skill level of the student, but basic weekly lessons with a rented horse are $35 per hour, including equipment. Special activities include birthday parties, hayrides, retreats, and 4-H programs. Family outings are encouraged so that all members of the family are introduced gently to the horses and equipment, becoming "horse friendly" before actually riding. Mother-and-child(ren) outings, for example, are popular. A certified instructor for children with special needs, Bunnie Graham, and others provide a quality program for riders with disabilities. From IH 35 take Dessau Road east around the Dessau Dance Hall to Gregg Lane. Go east on Gregg Lane, when it dead-ends at Cameron Road turn left, take the first entrance on the left. The address is 13404 Cameron Road, Manor, Texas, 78653.

Medway Ranch (263-5151) south of Lakeway is uniquely situated in a bend of Lake Austin. This Hill Country ranch with 400 acres offers outstanding scenery as well as a full line of services: children's activities, hayrides, birthday parties and even weddings. There is something for everyone. The core business consists of boarding, training, scenic trail rides, and riding lessons. Rates are by the hour. Scenic trail rides leave every 2 hours starting at

10 a.m. or as scheduled by reservation. From Austin take RM 2222 west to RM 620. Go left on RM 620 toward Lakeway. The Lakeway water tower—disguised as a golf ball—becomes visible ahead on the right shortly before you must get into the left lane, from which you turn onto Murfin Road and follow it about 1.5 miles to Pecan Road. Drive on to Medway Ranch. Address: 13500 Pecan Drive, Austin, Texas, 78734.

Belle Terre Equestrian Center (259-1620) has a limited number of rental horses available for lessons, but the scenery is beautiful, especially the foliage in autumn. And the location at 6734 Spicewood Springs Road is convenient to northwest residents.

Travelers preparing for that next jaunt to remote areas of foreign countries may wish to contact **Fairhaven Stables at** 928-9979 or at P.O. Box 5697, Austin, Texas, 78763. Fairhaven offers a full line of services, including boarding, training, and lessons, but specializes in teaching the novice how to "rough it" on horseback in remote areas of third-world countries.

PUBLICATIONS

Goldman, Mary Elizabeth. *The Trail Rider's Guide to Texas.* Plano, Texas: Woodware Publishing, Republic of Texas Press, 1993.

Kwalwasser, Amy, and Carolyn Banks. *The Horse Lover's Guide to Texas.* Austin, Texas: Texas Monthly Press, 1988. Lists stables, trainers, and other important information by county.

▮ Wildlife and Rehabilitation

The habitat, geology, and topography of Central Texas plus the springs around Austin and San Marcos make the area suitable for an unusually high number of rare species. This may be one reason the U.S. Fish and Wildlife Service maintains an office in Austin. Particularly well known in our area are 2 songbirds, the Black-capped Vireo and the Golden-cheeked Warbler, that are endangered. Both birds suffer from loss of habitat through development and ranching and from competition and parasitism from the brown-headed cowbird. One of the city's newest preserves, Vireo Preserve, was explicitly designed to protect the Black-capped Vireo. The only breeding ground for the Black-capped Vireo and Golden-cheeked Warbler is right here in the Austin area, west of town.

Some species are found only in west Austin because of the dramatic change in topography between the Edwards Plateau and the Blackland Prairie. Examples are the giant desert centipede, attaining a length of up to 10 inches, and the Texas alligator lizard. Caves in the Hill Country are home to many rare invertebrates, and aquifer springs provide a pristine habitat for such rare amphibians as the Barton Springs salamander. This appropriately named salamander lives solely in Barton Springs. Its population has dropped sharply since the early 1970s. An October 1992 census found that the salamander inhabited an area a mere 5 square yards in size, compared to an area of 400 square yards in 1987. But changes in the way Barton Springs Pool is maintained may help save the salamander, which awaits possible listing by the U.S. Fish and Wildlife Service as an endangered species.

Another rare creature is the Houston toad, which lives among the Lost Pines of **Bastrop State Park**. A small pond there is one of the few places in all the world where this toad makes its home. The Texas Parks and Wildlife Department has conducted tours of this ecosystem under its Texas Conservation Passport program.

Good sources of information on rare species in the Austin area include the wildlife coordinator at the Austin Nature Center (327-8181), the University of Texas Zoology Department, Southwest Texas State University in San Marcos, and the Texas Parks and Wildlife Department (especially the endangered resources branch).

A species that is often unnecessarily feared is the bat. This nocturnal creature is the focus of Bat Conservation International (327-9721), based right here in Austin. From about March until November, people gather at dusk at the *Austin American -Statesman* building in downtown Austin to see hundreds of thousands of Mexican Free-tailed Bats fly out from under the Congress Avenue bridge over the Colorado River. Caves in the Hill Country are also known for exit flights of bats by the million.

The Golden-cheeked Warbler as well as other species can be seen at a 600-acre preserve in northwest Travis County owned by the Travis Audubon Society. Nonmembers must be accompanied by a member. The Travis Audubon Society, which conducts field trips to this preserve and other places, holds its general meeting the third Thursday of each month. Membership benefits include a subscription to the monthly newsletter *Signal Smoke* and the national magazine *Audubon*.

The Austin Nature Center, adjacent to 2 ponds and surrounded by native vegetation on an 80-acre preserve, is a good place to see animals that were brought in injured and have been rehabilitated and orphaned animals that cannot be returned to the wild. Included in the outdoor wildlife exhibits are owls and other birds of prey. Known as Zilker Preserve, this area is often used to teach children and the general public about nature. A variety of programs are offered. (See Chapter 1, *In the Heart of the City*, where the Austin Nature Center is first described for more information.)

Many injured or orphaned animals are found in and around Austin each year by people who do not know how to help them. Fortunately, they can turn to a volunteer organization called Wildlife Rescue, an association of caring people dedicated to raising, rehabilitating, and returning animals to the wild. The animals being rehabilitated are kept as independent as possible to avoid turning them into pets, thus giving them the best possible chance of surviving once they are released. Because of a shortage of volunteers as compared to the number of calls received, it is best to leave seemingly orphaned or uninjured wild animals alone. Only if there is obviously a problem should a human intervene. If you think an animal is in trouble, call 472-WILD to get additional information. They furnish general animal-care information to the public and place needy animals with trained Wildlife Rescue members. Until help can be arranged, keep the animal in a warm, dark, and quiet place. Thanks for caring about Austin's wildlife!

PUBLICATIONS

Graham, Gary L. *Texas Wildlife Viewing Guide.* Helena, Montana: Falcon Press Publishing, 1992. Published in cooperation with Defenders of Wildlife, this guide can be obtained from the Texas Parks and Wildlife Department. It is easy to use, includes tips on wildlife in every part of the state, and contains beautiful photographs and helpful maps.

Miller, Dorcas. *Track Finder.* Berkeley, California: Nature Study Guild, 1981. This handy pocket-sized book is one of a series of Finder books that make it easy to identify nature's flora and fauna. The book begins with the basic features of tracks that distinguish one kind from another and guides you to different pages of the book depending on the track features that you see.

In Tune with Nature

7

■ Wildflowers

Texas is world renowned for its spring wildflowers. The variety of habitats and soil conditions, pronounced rainfall difference from east to west, and moderate temperature gradient from north to south all contribute to a spring diversity unparalleled in the United States. The fields of bluebonnets, Indian paintbrushes, and other flowers capture the essence of Texas as no other sight does!

Wildflower blooming depends on many factors: severity of winter weather, amount and timing of rain and sunshine in the spring, and date of the last freeze. Usually spring blooming commences in mid to late February with redbuds, violets, and perhaps even a few precocious bluebonnets. Bluebonnets are in full bloom by mid-to late March. In general, increasing temperatures as we move into the summer favor the sunflower family, most of whose members are yellowish. For color variety, then, the prime time is April and early May, while earlier or later in the year one can see impressive displays of a particular species, such as bluebonnets in March or Indian blankets in June.

Wildflowers are easy to view along many of the major highways in the Texas Hill Country, thanks to the beautification program started by Lady Bird Johnson. Her efforts led to the establishment of the **National Wildflower Research Center** (292-4100) in 1982. NWRC is the *only* national nonprofit environmental organization dedicated to the preservation and reestablishment of native plants in natural and planned landscapes. Environmentally conscious construction was a paramount objective in the development of the gardens and buildings. Extensive planting of native species, the rooftop water harvesting system (the largest in North America), passive solar heating, breezeways, and use of recycled materials helped protect the Texas Hill Country ecosystem. Friendly, dedicated volunteers answer questions and help expand our knowledge of our "inherited garden"—the wildflowers. The center offers a wildflower viewing update from mid-March to the end of May through the **Wildflower Hotline** (832-4059 ext. 4). Call the NWRC to see where the best spots are for viewing from a car or on foot. Visit the center for on-site demonstrations and information on starting your own wildflower garden. Walk through the wildflower plots and feel the beauty that the first Texas pioneers experienced.

NWRC was located east of Austin on FM 973 until the spring of 1995. NWRC is now nestled on 42 acres south of Austin at 4801 La Crosse Boulevard—just 15 minutes from downtown. Go 0.9 miles south of the MoPac-Slaughter intersection (4.6 miles south of the MoPac-U.S. Highway 290 intersection), turn left at the NWRC sign. The grounds are open year-round Tuesday through Sunday 9 a.m. to 5:30 p.m. They are closed to the public on Mondays, and they are closed Labor Day, July 4th, Thanksgiving Day, Christmas Eve Day, Christmas Day, and New Year's Day. The center sponsors Wildflower Days in mid-April. NWRC conducts research in wildflower ecology and physiology and maintains a clearinghouse for the public on wildflower cultivation and conservation. One of the center's goals is to promote wildflowers in every yard and garden and along the roadways to ensure their survival over exotics, which are harder to care for and use more water. The center serves all of the United States and has brochures available on all areas. There is an admission charge.

The Texas Department of Transportation has seeded wildflowers along many of our major highways. In the spring look for beautiful displays along U.S. Highway 290 west to Fredericksburg and east to Giddings, Texas Highway 71 west to Llano and east to La Grange, and U.S. Highway 183 south to Corpus Christi. Loop 360 on the west side is also beautiful.

It is a real joy to travel on the back roads by car or bicycle. Since the wildflowers here are not seeded, the displays are patchier, but the diversity is much greater and the "hot spots" vary from year to year, making their discovery more satisfying. Texas may have the best system of back roads in the United States—well-paved, very lightly traveled, and relaxing. It appears that in wet years the spring wildflowers are best to the southeast, while in dry years the roads west of Austin are more impressive. If you decide to travel the back roads of Texas, the atlas *The Roads of Texas,* published by Shearer Publishing, is extremely useful.

Official wildflower trails and associated festivals include:

- Highland Lakes Bluebonnet Trail in the Hill Country, in Marble Falls during April (512/793-2803)

- Willow City Loop in Willow City (see *Bicycling* in Chapter 3).

The choice areas where almost any back road is worth exploring are:

- Northeast Area bounded by U.S. Highway 290 on the south (from Elgin east to Giddings), U.S. Highway 77 on the east (from Giddings north to Lexington), FM 112 on the north (from Lexington west to Taylor), and Texas Highway 95 on the west (from Taylor south back to Elgin)

- East Area bounded by Texas Highway 71 (from La Grange east to Columbus) and U.S. Highway 90 (from Columbus east to Sealy) on the south, Texas Highway 36 on the east (from Sealy north to Brenham), U.S. Highway 290 on the north (from Brenham west to Giddings), and U.S. Highway 77 on the west (from Giddings south back to La Grange)

- Southeast Area bounded by Texas Highway 71 on the north (from Austin east to La Grange), U.S. Highway 77 on the east (from La Grange south to Hallettsville), U.S. Highway 90A (Alternate) on the south (from Hallettsville west to Gonzales) and U.S. Highway 183 on the west (from Gonzales north through Luling and Lockhart back to Austin)

- Southwest Area bounded by IH 35 on the east (from Austin to New Braunfels), FM 306 on the southwest (from New Braunfels to U.S. Highway 281 south of Blanco), U.S. Highway 281 on the west (going north through Blanco), and U.S. Highway 290 on the north (going east back to Austin)

- West Area bounded by Texas Highway 71 on the northeast (west of Austin go along Texas Highway 71 from U.S. Highway 281 northwest almost to Brady), U.S. Highway 377 on the west (from just south of Brady to Mason), U.S. Highway 87 on the southwest to Fredericksburg, U.S. Highway 290 on the south to Johnson City, and U.S. Highway 281 on the east. This area includes the famous Willow City Loop.

- Northwest Area bounded by U.S. Highway 183 on the northeast to Lampasas, U.S. Highway 281 on the west to Marble Falls, and RM 1431 on the south to Cedar Park

Learning to identify wildflowers can be a pleasurable hobby and an important step to understanding the ecology of a region. For beginners, it is usually easiest to use a wildflower book that is arranged by color. Eventually, however, you will find it far more useful to identify wildflowers according to the scheme botanists use in which species are grouped into a genus and genera are grouped into families. For example, the Texas bluebonnet is in the genus "*lupinus*," which includes the "lupines," which are widely distributed in the United States. The lupines belong to the plant family "*leguminosae*" or legumes, which include peas, beans, mimosas, mesquites, and redbuds. The legume family is one of the largest and most widely distributed families in the world, as is the sunflower family, mentioned in paragraph one of this article. With a little practice and determination, you can begin to identify the characteristics that all members of a family have in common. A family approach to wildflower identification gives you the ability to determine the general affinity of wildflowers you see anywhere in the country (and indeed much of the world).

PUBLICATIONS

Ajilvsgi, Geyata. *Wildflowers of Texas*. Fredericksburg, Texas: Shearer Publishing, 1984. Arranged by color and within color by family, this publication provides good descriptions and photographs.

Enquist, Marshall. *Wildflowers of the Texas Hill Country*. Austin, Texas: Lone Star Botanical, 1987. Arranged by plant families, this book displays outstanding photographs. It is the *only* comprehensive book for the Hill Country.

Loughmiller, Campbell, and Lynn Loughmiller.*Texas Wildflowers*. Austin, Texas: University of Texas Press, 1984. Arranged by families, this book contains photographs of high quality.

Niehaus, T. F. *Field Guide to Southwestern and Texas Wildflowers*. Boston, Massachusetts: Houghton Mifflin, 1984. Arranged by color and within color by number of parts and flower shape, this guide has drawings and a key to the plant families at the back of the book. It is the best book for the southwest as a whole.

Tull, Delana, and G. O. Miller. *Field Guide to Wildflowers, Trees, and Shrubs of Texas*. Houston, Texas: Gulf Publishing, 1991. This field guide is the best for coverage of all flora—trees, shrubs and wildflowers—and keys are provided.

Wills, Mary Motz, and Howard S. Irwin. *Roadside Flowers of Texas.*
Austin, Texas: University of Texas Press, 1961. Arranged by
families, this source has drawings of the whole plant: flowers,
leaves, stems, and habit.

■ Gardens

For the most garden varieties in Austin you should go to **Zilker
Botanical Gardens** (477-8672) to enjoy 22 acres of plants and
flowers, which include a xeriscape garden, cactus garden, organic
garden, rose garden, oriental garden, fragrance garden, and butterfly trail. Guided group butterfly tours are available with advance
notice. The various gardens integrate flowers, shrubs, handsome
trees, natural grottoes, and fountains with lagoons into a design
that creates an environment of inspiration, beauty, and tranquility.
Educational opportunities for people of all ages are offered through
displays, research programs, and specialized gardens.

One of the specialized gardens is the **Xeriscape Demonstration
Garden**. It showcases the 7 xeriscape principles: reduce turf, use
native and low-water-use plants, improve the soil, water efficiently,
practice good maintenance, use mulch, and use good landscape
design. The garden displays over 50 native and low-water-use
plants, including trees, shrubs, ground covers, and wildflowers.
This garden is maintained by the Xeriscape Garden Club. This club
meets monthly on the third Wednesday at 7:30 p.m. at the Austin
Area Garden Center, 2220 Barton Springs Road. Call 370-9505 for
information.

The **Taniguchi Oriental Garden** is a special 3-acre area created
by Isamu Taniguchi over an 18-month period with no pay. He
dedicated it to the city of Austin and the University of Texas in
appreciation for the help given to his family. The oriental garden is
a delicate balance between earth and water. This peaceful garden
includes an authentic teahouse with a great view of downtown and
a "bridge to walk over the moon." This bridge provides the perfect
spot to admire the more than 22 lotus blooms that grace the pools of
water, and it personifies the poetic sensitivity of the ancient Orient.
The honeycombed rock lining the waterfalls and pathways throughout the garden are native, having come from the Lake Travis area.

The **Mable Davis Rose Garden**—an All-American Rose Garden—offers a display of labeled climbing and bush roses (over 800). The best bloom displays are April to June, and again in October.

One of the newest additions to Zilker Gardens is the **Douglas Blachly Butterfly Trail,** which includes a butterfly open-air hatchery. This trail and garden has been filled with local flowers and plants that attract numerous species of Texas butterflies, providing visitors with a view of many of Austin's beautiful species as well as migrating varieties. Guided tours feature the interaction between insects and plants in an ecosystem.

There are 44 garden groups that hold their meetings at the Austin Area Garden Center. Call for information on specific areas of interest. Many of these groups have special shows throughout the year. The Florarama Festival, usually held in May, the Spring Rose Show, and the Bonsai show are only a few examples of what the Austin Area Garden Center has to offer.

A great example of xeriscape gardening can be found in **Umlauf Sculpture Gardens** at 605 Robert E. Lee Road (445-5582). Several paths take you through the garden to discover over 130 sculptures by Charles Umlauf, an internationally recognized sculptor. Sculptures range from detailed realism to lyrical abstractions. Family groups, animals, religious and mythological figures, and nudes are featured in the collection. The figures are crafted from wood, terra cotta, stone, bronze, and marble. This serene and shady spot is wonderful for escaping the Austin summer heat while still communing with nature and art. A stream runs through the garden, forming small pools at various spots. Both the museum and the garden are accessible to people with disabilities.

The **Capitol Trail of Trees** is a fun and educational way of taking a walk while experiencing a little Texas history at the same time. The century-old Texas Capitol has long been recognized for the beauty of its grounds. From the earliest plantings, an effort has been made to display a diverse variety of native and exotic trees adapted to Texas. This small forest, while serving its traditional landscape functions, also acts as a useful arboretum for teaching, research, and observation. Because of the restoration of the Capitol, the guidebook for this trail is being revised and reprinted; call PARD to see if it is available.

There are 3 other Trails of Trees: **Stacy Park Trail of Trees** (lists 30 species of trees); **Zilker Park Trail of Trees** (lists 28 species of trees); and **Catherine Lamkin Arboretum Trail of Trees** along Boggy Creek (lists 35 species of trees). Guides for these trails are available from PARD.

Mayfield Park, as the name indicates, is actually a park, but the Cottage Gardens and the setting, complete with fountains and peacocks, call for it to be included in this section as well. Located at 3505 West 35th Street, this park offers garden plots, and the current ones feature herb, heritage flowers, and scent gardens.

Austin Community Gardens (458-2009), at 4814 Sunshine Drive, provides garden plots and technical and educational assistance in gardening to the community. Its Greenspot Program helps to create neighborhood gardens in low-income areas. With over 23 sites, Austin Community Gardens has some 700 clients who produce over 87,000 pounds of fresh produce. The sites are located at elementary schools, apartments, senior retirement centers, housing facilities for the homeless, and institutions for people with mental and physical disabilities, among other places.

Wells Branch Community Garden (251-0890), near Wells Branch Elementary School, is an organic garden where plots are available for $35 or $25 in two sizes, 20 x 20 ft. or 10 x 20 ft. Water is available and a tools co-op is on the site.

As a symbol of peace and friendship between America and Japan, and out of admiration for Admiral Nimitz, the people of Japan built and paid for the Garden of Peace at the **Admiral Nimitz State Historical Park** in Fredericksburg (210/997-4379). This garden incorporates the beautiful features of the classic Japanese garden, including a replica of Admiral Togo's study, built in Japan and reassembled in Fredricksburg. Benches along the tree-lined walk allow you to rest and contemplate the beauty before you.

The **San Antonio Botanical Gardens** (210/821-5143), at 555 Funston Place, are comprised of a variety of gardens, a conservatory, and historical structures. Below are listed only a few of the main features.

The **Lucille Halsell Conservatory** is an award-winning underground garden where plants are shielded from the harsh Texas weather. The New York designer, Emilio Ambasz, created a cluster of diamond- and cone-shaped domes that crown the conservatory and lend it the look of a futuristic city. These glassed-in pavilions allow sunlight to filter into the underground plant world and provide a majestic sense of space. Many worlds inhabit this underground garden, each with its own climate and category of plant life. From the arid Desert Pavilion where prickly cacti thrive, to the frigid Alpine Room with its mountain-loving edelweiss, the conservatory re-creates environments from around the world.

This "paradise of plant life" includes many rare, endangered, and costly specimens. It took many years to assemble the conservatory collection and thousands of road miles to nurseries all over the nation. As you walk into the conservatory, the first room, the Exhibition Room, serves as an introductory plant showcase for visitors. The foliage here undergoes 6 makeovers every year reflecting the seasons and holidays.

There are 5 other main display areas. The Alpine Room is a computer-controlled slice of mountain plant life where ground-hugging species rustle in the cold artificial wind. It is the only public exhibition of its type in the United States. The Desert Pavilion has still, dry air and houses such endangered species as elephants foot, as well as 20-foot saguaro cacti. The steamy Hot Tropical House and the Palm House transport you to an island setting, while the lush, overgrown Fern Room becomes mystical and damp.

Outside areas consist of a **sunken pond** and plaza surrounded by glass-domed chambers and an **orangerie** with its collection of tropical fruit-bearing trees in pots from Mexico. Over 30 acres of beautiful native Texas flora are set in faithful re-creations of their natural environments. Paths are easy to walk on as they wind through varying minilandscapes and ponds. Water foul and other small animals are often sighted as you share this unique habitat with them.

Another beautiful section of the San Antonio Botanical Gardens is the **Japanese Garden**, built to commemorate goodwill and friendship as a sister city with Kumamoto, Japan. Experience rustic simplicity in this re-creation of a traditional tea garden, which provides a site for people to perform the tea ceremony. The features that make this a wonderful garden stroll are large and small waterfalls, an island, bamboo hills, and a meditation stone, placed around a pond. In addition, numerous beautiful small hills were created. Among these, 2 hills represent San Antonio and Kumamoto. Eternal ties between the 2 cities are expressed by the double stone bridge in the center of the garden.

Many programs and volunteer opportunities exist at the gardens. Call for information. If you have a strong interest in gardens, be sure to see this one!

■ Nature Photography

Unlike most metropolitan areas, Austin offers the nature photographer limitless opportunities to discover and record natural phenomena. Mild temperatures throughout the year, a long growing season, and an unusual geographic location contribute to this accessibility. In addition, the area's many parks and natural areas provide just the setting for this exciting pastime.

To many observers, nature photography implies only wildlife photos. Though wildlife is an integral part of nature, it actually represents only 1 area of concentration possible in this part of the country. Plant, insect, and landscape subjects also abound in the Austin area. The following are just a few of the many locations in which viewing our natural world through the lens of a camera can be enjoyed throughout the year.

Many varieties of wildflowers and the insects attracted to them can be found at **McKinney Falls State Park,** especially several cacti that bloom in early to midsummer. For those interested in bird photography, this is a good place in early summer to find the multicolored Painted Bunting, and Screech Owls have been observed posing patiently among the forest branches during the day. The topography of this 640-acre area in southeast Austin was shaped by ancient volcanic eruptions and by Onion Creek, which carves its way through the park, tumbling over ledges and building sandbars. Bald cypress along the creek is the most prominent tree, but you also find live oaks, mesquite, and all the usual understory trees and shrubs associated with riverine habitat in Central Texas.

Lamar Boulevard follows the contours of **Shoal Creek** between 12th and 29th Streets in central Austin. Hike-and-bike trails

provide immediate access to many miles of the creek. In addition to reflecting pools and gigantic boulders, the photographer can find a profusion of blooming trees along the creek in the spring. Redbud, wild plum, mesquite, and peach take turns stunning the viewer from March through May.

Westcave Preserve (210/825-3442), located about 20 miles west of Austin off Texas Highway 71, is a collapsed grotto with a small cave still adjacent, complete with cave bacon formations. A spectacular wispy waterfall and travertine pools greet the visitor at the end of the path that ambles through the perennial creek's canyon. Meticulously protected ferns, columbines, native orchids, and aquatic life abound as one nears the falls. Tours are given, weather permitting, on Saturdays and Sundays every 2 hours from 10 a.m. to 4 p.m. for a maximum of 30 people, and reservations are not taken. Access is available only on the scheduled tours. Sunlight on the falls is normally best around 10 a.m.

On the way to Westcave, **Hamilton Pool Preserve** (512/264-2740) offers more interesting photo opportunities, as well as a chance to get wet and picnic by the pool or along the creek. Located downstream and on the opposite side of the Pedernales River from Westcave, Hamilton Pool is administered by Travis County. There is an entry fee and reservations are preferred, since access is limited in order to reduce human impact on a sadly misused area.

Nature photographers in Austin are fortunate to have a conifer forest within 30 miles of downtown Austin. The Lost Pines at **Bastrop State Park** (512/321-2101) are a definite contrast to the rest of Central Texas's flora. Mushroom photography can be enjoyed here in the spring and midfall, and wildflowers abound in the spring. A large pond surrounded by tall trees harbors several varieties of ducks and other waterfowl in the winter.

Wild Basin Wilderness Preserve (327-7622), a 227-acre wilderness on Loop 360 saved several years ago from urban development, is a veritable gold mine for the nature photographer. The area is typically "hill country" and offers abundant plant and animal life. Deer, squirrel, turkey, and armadillo are just a few of the wildlife species that live here. The elusive Black-capped Vireo is one of the rarer examples of birdlife that make Wild Basin home. The area abounds in plant and insect life adapted to both semiarid and aquatic environments, since both conditions exist here. The preserve is open from sunrise to sunset daily, and tours are available from 10:00 to 11:30 a.m. on Saturdays and from 1:00 to 2:30 p.m. on Sundays.

One final word about shooting landscapes in and around Austin. At first glance, there may appear to be nothing spectacular about the Hill Country terrain. There are no overwhelming topographic features such as can be found in Colorado or Utah. Rather, the Hill Country presents a great challenge to the photographer, compelling one to see that which is simple, direct, and strong in the terrain. Photographers must extract that which is relevant and important in their approach to this area of the state. Powerful landscapes comparable to scenery anywhere exist here, but they are not easily captured. Sometimes it may require waiting for just the right light or maybe a mist. In short, nature photography in Austin and the surrounding area is accessible yet demanding and, more often than not, a great challenge for creative growth with a camera.

PUBLICATIONS

Fitzharris, Tim. *The Sierra Club Guide to 35 Millimmeter Landscape Photography*. San Francisco, California: Sierra Club, 1994.

Kodak. *More Joy of Photography*. Redding, Massachusetts: Addison-Wesley, 1988. A good guide for the photographer, especially a beginner.

Kreh, Lefty. *The L. L. Bean Guide to Outdoor Photography*. New York, New York: Random, 1988. This is specifically about photographing nature.

▌Geology

Our forefathers selected Austin, then a hamlet called Waterloo, as the capital of Texas, because its unique geological features set it apart from other centrally located areas. Within a few miles of the capital, fertile, well-watered prairies and high-plateau grasslands beckoned farmers and ranchers. Wooded bottomlands of the Colorado River and extensive outcroppings of limestone provided a ready source of quality building materials, and many cool springs, creeks, and the Colorado River ensured plenty of water even in the driest years. Even the first-time visitor to Austin notices the marked differences between the Blackland Prairies to the east and the dry, ruggedly scenic, rocky highlands to the west of the city.

The topography changes abruptly because of extensive cracking, or faulting, of the underlying rocks. The major fault lines run from northeast to southwest across most of the state, roughly parallel here with IH 35. The fault system, called the Balcones Fault Zone, formed at least 12 million years ago after developing for several million years. It has remained stable since then, and Austin is considered safe from earthquakes. Land along the fault zone to the west was uplifted, land to the east subsided. Ages of erosion wore away sedimentary rock at the surface on both sides of the fault zone, but the loss was greatest on the east side. Despite subsequent buildup of rock-forming sediments in later ages, there remains a substantial difference in elevation between east Austin and west Austin. That difference averages 300 feet; at Mount Bonnell, it exceeds 1,000 feet.

Rainfall soaking into the ground works its way through fractures in the rock, dissolving minute amounts of limestone as it passes through. Over the eons, the cracks enlarge, especially in spots of softer stone, becoming conduits for ever-increasing quantities of water. Eventually, the water reaches relatively impermeable layers of rock that it cannot penetrate so readily. It accumulates in large quantities in the rock layers just above the impermeable rock. These water-bearing layers may take the form of limestone honeycombed with irregular channels and caverns containing water, or they may be water-soaked sandstone or sands and gravels. Whatever, these water-bearing layers, or aquifers, tapped by wells, supply a great deal of fresh, high-quality water for human use. Underground water is Austin's most valuable natural resource.

In large areas along the Balcones Fault Zone, Cretaceous rocks of the Edwards Formation have been exposed. At these places, rainwater (and any other fluids or soluble materials, if dumped or spilled) can flow into the Edwards aquifer. In other places, faulting allows cool, refreshing springs to gush forth from the aquifer. Barton Springs in Austin, Comal Springs in New Braunfels, and the San Marcos Springs (Aquarena Springs) in San Marcos offer cool respite from summer's heat, swimming, and water play to residents and visitors, many of whom choose to stay. Lesser springs, the source of many clear-flowing creeks, dot the countryside, providing numerous swimming holes and recreational opportunities throughout the area.

The clear waters of the Colorado River and its tributaries cut through this rugged terrain; all the more so when moisture in warm gulf breezes is forced to rise above the Balcones Escarpment and the highlands to the west, suddenly condensing in the world-class torrential cloudbursts so familiar to Central Texans. The resulting rain-scoured, white limestone creekbeds flowing with crystal-clear streams lend special charm to the picturesque Central Texas scene.

Over long geologic ages the molten surface of the planet cooled, and erosion wore down the high places and built up sediment in the low places; all the while volcanic and tectonic forces raised up mountains and continents. In Central Texas, the base of igneous rock was overlain again and again with sediments later eroded away or remelted by heat and pressure to form metamorphic rocks. None of the sediments laid down in past ages persisted until conditions in the Cretaceous Period (about 137 to 65 million years ago) favored the deposition of limestone. At that time, Central Texas was covered by shallow inland seas, sometimes deeper, sometimes marshy and very shallow. Abundant marine life consisted largely of organisms with calcium carbonate shells. As these creatures lived and died by the billions over millions of years, their shells accumulated at the bottom of the sea. These sediments eventually hardened into the thick layers of limestone that cover Central Texas. The Balcones Fault formed when these limestone layers cracked under the weight of massive overlaid sedimentary deposits along the Gulf Coast. Because they remained relatively unchanged by heat and pressure, these extensive rock layers provide a fairly good fossil record of Earth's history.

Most rock outcroppings in the Austin area are Cretaceous limestones. At **Pilot Knob** to the southeast, an extinct volcano of the Cretaceous Period produced deposits of ash and volcanic rock. An ancient beach formed around the mound of volcanic material has become limestone, visible at McKinney Falls State Park. An outcropping of volcanic rock similar to that in the volcano itself occurs along the roadside about 2/3 of a mile east of the intersection of Bluff Springs Road and Elroy Road. It probably formed as a lava flow.

The widespread, thick beds of Cretaceous limestone covering the Austin area contain many marine fossils and a few wetlands fossils, such as dinosaur tracks. Happily, dinosaur tracks were recently discovered in Zilker Park! Nearly every excavation made in the local limestones uncovers interesting fossils, some quite extraordinary. Check out the major excavations at highway construction sites as well as the lesser ones for new streets and subdivisions. Hunting for fossils along the roadsides is acceptable as long as you observe traffic safety precautions. Remember to ask for permission from private property owners. *The City of Austin prohibits removal of fossil materials from the parks and greenbelts.* Shoal Creek and other creekbeds cutting through the limestone contain many good specimens to study in place.

At least 2 amateur groups study paleontology and conduct field trips in the Austin area. The Austin Paleontological Society meets on the third Tuesday of each month except July (when the club has a picnic) and December (when it has a Christmas party) at Murchison Community School, Room 114, 3700 North Hills Drive, at 7:00 p.m. There is a membership fee per year for an individual or family. Dues may be mailed to the Society in care of the Treasurer,

1603 Twilight Ridge, Austin, Texas, 78746. Phone 452-7325 or 327-4005 for more information. For information on the Central Texas Paleontological Society, call Don O'Neill at 251-2848.

Besides limestone (primarily calcite, made of calcium carbonate) and the related dolomite (magnesium replacing the calcium), other rocks and minerals worth noting also occur in Travis County. Celestite of gem-quality blue is found at Mount Bonnell and other places west of Austin. As crystalline masses in limestone, celestite occurs widely and is easy to see in water-scoured limestone beds, such as the South San Gabriel River bed at U.S. Highway 183 north of Leander. Calcite crystals, gypsum (calcium sulfate), pyrite, marcasite, basalt and its component minerals, tuff, bentonite, shales, chert, and sandstones occur in Travis County. Pebbles of many other minerals and rocks, washed downriver from the Llano Uplift area, may be found in gravel along the Colorado River.

A bit farther afield, but still within an easy day's drive of Austin, the Llano Uplift beckons. Molten granite rock intruded (welled up beneath, but did not surface) beneath the older metamorphic rocks around Llano about a billion years ago. Though many sedimentary layers of rock formed above the granite in succeeding ages, the continuing uplift of the area accelerated erosion, leaving large areas of bare granite exposed. Very old and diverse rocks dating from the Precambrian Period form outcrops at various points around the edges of the Uplift. A trip from the Upper Cretaceous (100 million years old) rocks of the Austin area to the ancient Precambrian rocks of Llano lets you review the geological record of 500 million years! The Llano Uplift is a great place for collectors. Llanite, a unique granite containing blue quartz crystals (due to chromium impurities), occurs nowhere else in the world.

The granite dome of **Enchanted Rock State Natural Area** (915/247-3903) formed as part of the Llano Uplift. Nearby counties offer opportunities to study the varied minerals of Texas, such as the famous gem-quality Texas topaz found in Mason County near Streeter, Grit, and Katemcy. Write or go by the Mason Chamber of Commerce, P.O. Box 156, 108 Fort McKavett, Mason, Texas, 76856, for information on local ranches that allow hunting for topaz, quartz, garnet, microcline, and other minerals.

Learn more about our Central Texas geology by joining one of the geology clubs in our area, such as the Austin Gem and Mineral

Society. For the meeting time, place, and dues, contact Mac Ellis, President, at 321-4703 or Route 3, Box 327, Bastrop, Texas, 78602.

The Williamson County Gem and Mineral Society meets regularly on the second Sunday of each month at the Chamber of Commerce Building, Stadium Drive at U.S. Highway 81 North, Georgetown, at 2:30 p.m. unless otherwise announced. Changes are made in the schedule for Mother's Day, the July Watermelon Cut, and Christmas. Address: P.O. Box 422, Georgetown, Texas, 78626.

Texas Memorial Museum (471-1604), on the University of Texas campus, has an excellent collection of geological specimens, including examples from our area, like the fossil *Mosasaur* found in Onion Creek. The **Geology Building** (471-5172), also on the UT campus, houses the Department of Geology and contains many displays and exhibits on Texas and local geology that provide a wealth of information for both amateur and professional geologists. The University of Texas also has the Bureau of Economic Geology (471-7721), University Station, Box X, Austin, Texas, 78713-7508. Write or stop by the Bureau in Building 130 at 10100 Burnet Road in Austin for a free list of B.E.G. publications, which include:

- Garner, L. E., and K. P. Young. *Environmental Geology of the Austin Area: An Aid to Urban Planning* (Report of Investigations 86: 1976).

- Girard, R. M. *Texas Rocks and Minerals: An Amateur's Guide* (Guidebook 6: 1964).

- King, E. A. Jr. *Texas Gemstones.* (Reportof Investigations Number 42: 1961).

- Matthews, W. H. III. *Texas Fossils: An Amateur's Handbook* (Guidebook 2: 1960).

- Proctor, C. V. Jr. *Geologic Atlas of Texas*, Austin Sheet (1974).

- Trippet, A. R. amd L. E. Garner. *Guide to Points of Geological Interest in Austin* (Guidebook 16: 1976).A highly recommended geological driving tour of Austin, with lots of stops at interesting sites and a good map.

The books listed below are available through the Austin Public Library, a good place to browse and pick a favorite. Outdoor recreation outfitters and local bookstores carry them as well. Outfitters emphasize publications on specific areas and specific activities: hiking or biking the Hill Country or scuba diving in Texas. Bookstores have a wider variety of more general-information publications, with a few of the specific ones included. The UT co-op has a very good selection with technical emphasis.

PUBLICATIONS

Peterson, J. F. *Enchanted Rock State Natural Area: A Guidebook to the Landforms*. San Antonio, Texas: Terra Cognita Press, 1988.

Spearing, Darwin. *Roadside Geology of Texas*, 4th ed. Missoula, Montana: Mountain Press Publishing, 1994.

■ Rocks and Fossils

Austin stone, limestone, and honeycomb rock are all the same sedimentary rock. Since Austin is situated on the edge of the Edwards Plateau, everywhere you look you can see limestone in some form. Look closely and you will see impressions made by sea creatures from the Cretaceous period. For a great place to study fossils, try **Pease Park** or **Wooten Park** along Shoal Creek, which parallels Lamar Boulevard. *The City of Austin prohibits removal of fossil materials from parks and greenbelts.* Many exyogera and gastropod fossils are washed into this area. Road cuts on **City Park Road** and **Loop 360** have clams, sea urchins, and ammonites. The **Big Walnut Creek Greenbelt** between Braker and Parmer Lanes reveals shark's teeth. **Smith's Branch** at Georgetown is another good hunting ground for shark's teeth, oysters, and brachiopods.

Take a walk along Barton Creek adjacent to Barton Springs. Barton Creek carves its way through the Edwards Plateau, which consists of thick limestone beds deposited by a shallow sea about 100 million years ago. When water dissolves this limestone it creates networks of caves and reservoirs underground with canyons and valleys at the surface. The Edwards Aquifer stores about 300,000 acre-feet of water that provides drinking water for an area stretching from San Antonio to Georgetown. As you drive along Loop 360 you may see signs indicating the aquifer recharge zone, a broad area wherein the watersheds of 5 creeks direct much surface water to percolate into the network of limestone channels that forms the Edwards Aquifer. Liquid or soluble substances left on the ground in this area could easily be washed by rain into the aquifer, which people must learn serves as a major source of drinking water for people and livestock. Careless mishandling of hazardous substances over the recharge zone can result in pollution of the aquifer.

Get acquainted with the wonderful outdoor treasures in and around Austin. The **Austin Nature Center** offers "Fossil Hunters for Grades 1-6," while the **Zilker Preserve** next to the Austin Nature Center has 80 acres of nature trails along the foot of limestone cliffs and a shady creek (no pets or bikes are permitted). Call 327-8181 for more information. **Wild Basin Preserve**, on Loop 360 about a mile north of Bee Caves Road, has over 2 miles of hiking trails along Bee Creek. It is open every day from sunrise to sunset, and tours are conducted 10 a.m. to 11:30 a.m. Saturday and 1 p.m. to 2:30 p.m. Sunday. Another good place is **McKinney Falls State Park**, at 7102 Scenic Loop Road, with over 3 miles of hike-and-bike trails and the half-mile Smith Rock Shelter. (See Chapter 2, *At the Park,* for more information about Wild Basin and McKinney Falls State Park.)

Hamilton Pool Preserve offers a guided tour each Saturday at 10 a.m. See the legendary collapsed grotto and hike the trail along the bald cypress-lined creek to the Pedernales River. There is a fee per car; the hours are 9 a.m. to 6 p.m. (no pets are allowed). See Chapter 2 or call 264-2740 for more information. Take Texas Highway 71 west 1 mile past RM 620, turn left on RM 3238 (Hamilton Pool Road), and go 13 miles to the entrance.

Farther west the great Llano Uplift consists of granite that comes from the earth's magma or igneous rock. **Enchanted Rock State Natural Area** (915/247-3903) is dominated by massive dome-shaped hills of pink granite. Take U.S. Highway 290 west to Fredericksburg and watch the road cuts along the way for examples of metamorphic rock (see Chapter 2, *At the Park,* for more information). Keep a record of what fossils you find and where. A good place to see fossil exhibits is the Texas Memorial Museum, to which we turn next.

PUBLICATIONS

Crow, Melinda. *The Rockhound's Guide to Texas.* Helena, Montana: Falcon Press Publishing, 1994.

Finsley, Charles. *A Field Guide to the Fossils of Texas.* Houston, Texas: Gulf Publishing, 1989.

▮ Texas Memorial Museum

The Texas Memorial Museum, an integral part of the University of Texas at Austin, is dedicated to the study and interpretation of the natural and social sciences, with emphasis on Texas, the Southwest, and Latin America. Included are the fields of geology, paleontology, zoology, botany, ecology, anthropology, and history. The museum is world renowned for its research collections, laboratories, exhibits, and programs. Several varieties of Texas limestone were used to construct the museum building.

Four floors are devoted to exhibits. At the entrance level, you find the original Goddess of Liberty, a 16-foot statue that stood atop the State Capitol dome for nearly a century. Geology and paleontology are represented by sparkling displays of gems, minerals, and rocks, plus an outstanding assemblage of Texas fossil vertebrates. Ancient amphibians and reptiles share space with giant Ice Age mammals. Preparation of the skeleton of the Onion Creek Mosasaur can be seen from the gallery.

Elsewhere in the museum life-size dioramas depict the life of Texas mammals, birds, and reptiles by day and by night. The distribution of this wildlife, region by region, is also covered. To highlight the major North American cultural groups, artifacts from prehistoric Indian sites throughout Texas are displayed.

A small building north of the museum entrance contains examples of dinosaur trackways. Imprinted in the bed of the Paluxy River near Glen Rose, Texas, these limestone blocks are 105 million years old. They were excavated from the river bed and placed on display at the museum in 1940.

The museum is open to the public 7 days a week during the following hours: Monday through Friday 9 a.m. to 5 p.m., Saturday 10 a.m. to 5 p.m., and Sunday 1 p.m. to 5 p.m. Groups are encouraged to visit, but tour reservations must be made in advance. Call 471-1605 or write to the museum at 2400 Trinity Street, Austin, Texas, 78705. Although contributions are encouraged, there is no entry fee.

■ Archaeology

Outdoor lovers were enjoying Central Texas long before Christopher Columbus stumbled on America: ancient cultures beat him to the New World by about 12,000 years. Archaeologists study these long-vanished peoples, their past life, and their remains. Like modern detectives, these scientists study vanished cultures by looking at details and artifacts at an ancient scene. Archaeology generally falls into 2 categories: *prehistoric archaeology*, which deals with evidence left by cultures who existed before people had a written language; and *historical archaeology*, which examines the remains of cultures that flourished when someone wrote about them.

Even though ancient Texans left behind a great deal of evidence, both historic and prehistoric, ordinary people rarely know how or where to look for it. And archaeologists want to keep it that way. Like onlookers who beat police to the scene of a crime, well-meaning sightseers who pick up an arrowhead or a burned stone before archaeologists have a chance to study it may remove evidence that the scientists need to reconstruct a vanished culture. So even though Central Texas abounds with sites that contain evidence of ancient lives, archaeologists usually discourage sightseers from looking for them. But if you have a yen for the distant past, don't despair: several intriguing archaeological sites in Central Texas happily welcome responsible and curious visitors.

The **Smith Rock Shelter Nature Trail** at **McKinney Falls State Park** leads to an overhanging rock shelf that was home to prehistoric Texans about 1,400 years ago. The same park contains an example of historical archaeology: the **McKinney Homestead**, built in the late 1800s, which has been thoroughly poked and prodded by archaeologists.

While you're enjoying frenetically beautiful **Aquarena Springs** in **San Marcos**, remember that ancient Texans enjoyed the springs too—as early as 11,000 years ago. **Spring Lake** now covers one of their ancient campsites. Archaeologists have to dive under water to study it. And think about this when lounging in **Barton Springs Pool**: it is a good bet that, wherever springs flow today, the remains of vanished Texans are nearby. Like us, they needed a steady water supply to survive.

Farther south, **San Antonio** abounds with historical archaeological sites dating from the early 1700s, including one of the most famous spots in Texas: the **Alamo**, a Spanish mission and monument to Texas independence, located at Alamo Plaza (210/225-1391). The **San Antonio Missions National Park** at 727 E. Durango Boulevard (210/229-5701) contains 5 other Spanish mission sites.

For a good book on Texas archaeology, try *A Field Guide to Archaeological Sites of Texas* by Parker Nunley. To learn more about archaeology in Central Texas, visit the **Texas Memorial Museum**, profiled earlier in this chapter; the **Witte Museum** at 3801 Broadway in San Antonio (210/820-2111); or the **University of Texas Institute of Texan Cultures** at 801 S. Bowie Street in San Antonio (210/558-2300). Or contact one of these organizations:

The Texas Archaeological Society
Center for Archaeological Research
University of Texas at San Antonio
San Antonio, Texas 78285

Travis County Archeological Society
10100 Burnet Road
Austin, Texas 78758-4497

Southern Texas Archaeological Association
123 E. Crestline
San Antonio, Texas 78201

■ Stargazing and Astronomy

UT star parties are held regularly, weather permitting. On Wednesdays, from sunset until about 10 p.m., small portable telescopes set up on the roof of UT's 14-story Robert Lee Moore Hall (26th and Speedway Street) permit observation of the moon, some planets, and bright star clusters. The rooftop view of the city, especially at sunset, and cool breezes add to the evening's enjoyment in warmer weather. In cool weather, take extra wraps. Wheelchair access is limited by a 1-foot step up to the roof level from the 14th floor. On Saturdays, 8 p.m. to 10 p.m. (sunset until 10:30 p.m. in summer), UT allows public access to the 9-inch telescope in **Painter Hall Observatory** on 24th Street, just northeast of the UT Tower (with no elevator, you have to climb the stairs to the fifth floor). This large telescope, despite the city glare and dust, still produces good images of planets and the closer, brighter, deep-space objects, such as the Great Nebula in Orion, the Ring and the Dumbbell Nebulae, and the Andromeda Galaxy.

Off-campus star parties are held at UT's **Bee Cave Research Center** (263-2189), 506 Crystal Creek Drive, off Bee Caves Road (RM 2244) near the dark of the moon. There a historic 12-inch Newtonian telescope, over 100 years old, which was given to UT by an accomplished French astronomer, still works very well. A 25-inch Cassegrain telescope once owned by the U.S. Air Force has not held up so well, but it can capture good images of the moon, bright planets, and bright deep-sky objects, such as star clusters and nebulae. The site is wheelchair accessible, but actual viewing through the eyepieces requires standing or climbing a stepladder. Again, the glare of city lights has compromised the effectiveness of the optics. It may be time to relocate the telescope farther away, out of the path of "progress," though a suitable dark-sky place will be hard to find and hard to fund as well. Meanwhile, the Bee Caves Road location has restrooms and some parking areas.

The Austin Astronomical Society meets on the second Friday of each month at Austin Community College, 12th and Rio Grande, Room 320, at 7:30 p.m. Members enjoy excellent, informative programs; following the regular meeting they often convene for discussion at a favorite pizza parlor. Contact the Society by mail at P.O. Box 12831, Austin, Texas, 78711. A newsletter and *Sky and Telescope Magazine* are included as a privilege of membership. Dues are collected in September and October, the magazine subscription running from December through the following November. For a small annual fee, members may operate the Society's 12.5-inch Newtonian telescope after instruction. Star parties are held monthly, on the weekend nearest the dark of the moon, often at the UT Bee Cave Research Center, where the telescope is permanently mounted, but sometimes also at nearby parks. Pedernales Falls State Park, for example, is popular. Occasional star parties are held farther afield. West Texas, especially the McDonald Observatory area at public viewing times, attracts many interested members. Guests and visitors are welcome.

The UT chapter of Students for the Exploration and Development of Space (UTSEDS) is affiliated with the American Astronautical

Society, which publishes up-to-date technical information, and with the Space Studies Institute, which conducts advanced research in space technology. Membership is limited to UT students. Dues are per semester. Nonstudents who donate $5 to the club may be placed on the club mailing list and attend meetings, lectures, and films as guests. For more information call 471-5284, or come to the Texas Union Building, Room 5.132, on the UT campus. Check the *Daily Texan* campus newspaper for announcements.

Have you ever seen a satellite whiz overhead? The Austin Space Frontier chapter of the National Space Society (c/o 12717 Bullick Hollow Road, Austin, Texas, 78726) is a public advocacy group dedicated to progress in space exploration and development. Special projects, exhibits, and other public education efforts promote public awareness of space-related issues. Need a speaker for your next club meeting? Members welcome the opportunity to speak on solar power and other space-related topics. A specialty of this group, satellite watches, must be carefully planned. Special software, used with data obtained periodically from the U.S. government, can predict the time a given satellite will appear. If your group would like to see, for example, the Russian MIR satellite, or the Hubble space telescope, allow up to 6 weeks to acquire data and run the program, and allow time for the satellite orbit to cross your part of the night sky. Remember, conduct satellite watches away from city lights, preferably in the darker phases of the moon.

FOR SPECIAL PEOPLE 8

▮ Children

For children, **Zilker Park** is a great place to start. According to a 1992 "Best for Families" survey by *Austin Child,* a parenting magazine, Zilker Park won in several categories, including best playground and best sunny day outing. Particularly popular with children are the spring-fed **Barton Springs Pool**, a train ride, and a playscape built in 1970. Renovated in the early 1990s, the playscape now has a phantom ship built around a tree and a fire escape surrounded by sand, both of which are accessible to children who use wheelchairs. The Zilker Park Dinosaur Trackways, which were discovered recently, are open for guided tours 9 a.m. to 11 a.m. Saturdays. Tours take 30-40 minutes, and visitors must wear soft-soled shoes. If interested, call 251-1816. Other favorites are feeding the ducks where Barton Creek flows into Town Lake, strolling through the **Zilker Gardens**, and bicycling the 8.5-mile **Town Lake Hike-and-Bike Trail**.

Zilker Hillside Theater, not far from Barton Springs Pool, provides concerts outdoors. Any concert outdoors is better for children who may not sit still, but **Symphony Square**, at Red River and 11th Streets, even offers concerts especially for children each Wednesday during the summer. An instrument petting zoo, magicians, singers, and dancers, or even a pied piper may be featured at these concerts. For information on these children's programs, call the Director of Education for the Austin Symphony Orchestra's Youth Programs at 476-6064.

Close to Zilker Park is the **Austin Nature Center** off Stratford Drive. Indoors, discovery boxes that are modeled after the Smithsonian Museum of Natural History show life in a variety of places, such as a cave or a tree. Outdoors, children can enjoy a pond, animals from the wild that are on exhibit, or several nice nature trails. The educational programs for children have catchy names like Wild about Wildlife, Babies and Beasties, and Wildlife Neighbors. The center is open 9 a.m. to 5 p.m. Monday through Saturday and noon to 5 p.m. Sunday. One particularly popular event is the annual Safari, which features a petting zoo, Indian Village, outdoor music, and many activities specifically for children.

The Austin Nature Center sponsors both summer and year-round programs for people in specific age ranges. For example, the center might offer Nature Magic for 4- and 5-year-olds, Discovery Nature for 6- to 12-year-olds, High Adventure for 10- to 13-year-olds, and Youth Urban Rangers for 15- to 18-year-olds. Some programs are specifically designed for school-aged youth whose life in the city limits their exposure to the outdoors. Activities for the younger children are usually on-site, while older youth may go canoeing, camping, or on other field trips. Many activities take place at the nature preserve close by or at other preserves farther out.

Two good places to take children and other special people are **Mayfield Park** and **Laguna Gloria**, located next to each other at the west end of 35th Street. Both have good trails for walking. Children especially like the peacocks at Mayfield Park, which has undergone considerable improvement and restoration in recent years. Laguna Gloria has a beautiful outdoor amphitheater next to a lagoon and offers art classes for children. Children especially like the activities at Fiesta, Laguna Gloria's annual art festival held the third weekend in May. Nearby is **Mount Bonnell**, where children can climb a staircase of 100 steps for a panoramic view of Austin. Also nearby is **Camp Mabry**, where children can explore planes, missiles, and tanks on permanent display, while others might enjoy the jogging trail.

The Parks and Recreation Department operates several recreation centers throughout town, some of which offer wading pools for the little kiddos or special interest classes for children. **Metz Park and Recreation Center** at 2407 Canterbury (478-8716), for example, has a wading pool and nature sanctuary. In northeast Austin, the **Dottie Jordan Park and Recreation Center** has wading pools, a hike-and-bike trail, and other facilities located along Little Walnut Creek. **Parque Zaragoza Recreation Center**, at 741 Pedernales in east Austin, has an outdoor theater, while the **South Austin Recreation Center**, at 1100 Cumberland (444-6601) off South 1st Street, has a playscape.

The **Jourdan-Bachman Pioneer Farm** (837-1215) in far north-east Austin, is a unique, living history museum depicting Nine-teenth-century farm life on 66 acres of scenic land, complete with live animals, blacksmithing, and vintage costumes. This a good place to take children anytime but especially when there are special events. Day camps feature hands-on "field to food" activities.

Wild Basin Wilderness Preserve (327-7622) is a 220-acre refuge along Loop 360 a mile north of Bee Caves Road (RM 2244). Operated by a nonprofit organization under contract with Travis County, the preserve offers outdoor education programs for children as well as adults. Regular guided tours inform visitors of the geology, water resources, plants, and animals of the Hill Country. The preserve also contains 2.5 miles of trails through woodlands, grasslands, and streamside habitats, including an easy-access trail designed for people with mobility impairments. (See Chapter 2, *At the Park,* for more information on Wild Basin Wilderness Preserve.)

The National Wildflower Research Center (WFRC) 292-4100 is a great place for children to see what native plants grow in this area. The WFRC will host classes especially for children.

The Capitol Area Council of the Boy Scouts offers programs in the 15 counties around Austin for boys 1st grade through 12th grade and for high school girls in the Explorers. There are 400 Cub Packs, Scout Troops, and Explorer Posts with 13,800 members. The Lone Star Girl Scout Council offers day camp in June at the Zilker Cabin and resident camp during the summer at Pace Bend Recreation Area. There are 15,000 girls active in the 18-county council.

Most chapters in this book contain activities in which children can participate. More information on horseback riding and other activities for children with disabilities is given in the next section.

PUBLICATIONS

Boyer, Robert E. *Austin Science Fun Guide*. Austin, Texas: College of Natural Sciences at the University of Texas at Austin, 1994.

Cornell, Joseph. *Sharing the Joy of Nature*. Nevada City, California: Dawn Publications, 1989. In this book and his earlier book, *Sharing Nature with Children,* Joseph Cornell describes great activities to do with children outdoors.

Crowell, Lynda, and Donna Nelson, eds. *Family Guide to Austin*. Austin, Texas: LCN, 1992. Write to LCN at 6626 Silvermine Drive, #100, Austin, Texas, 78736, or call 800/424-6291.

■ People with Disabilities

One of the biggest events held in Austin, usually toward the end of March, is the Capitol 10,000, a 6.2-mile run sponsored by the *Austin American-Statesman* in which accommodations are made for wheelchair athletes to participate. Many people with disabilities residing in Austin have excelled in one competitive sport or another.

One sport catching on, for example, is beep baseball for the blind or visually impaired. Austin's local team, the Austin Black Hawks, won the world championship in 1992. A sighted pitcher stands 20 feet from the batter. Since the two are on the same team, they try to work in tandem so the batter can hit the ball, which beeps 2 or 3 times per second. When the ball is hit out into the field, 6 field players on the opposite team try to grab the ball and hold it up before the batter makes it to the base. The base, like the ball, makes a sound that the batter can hear. If the batter touches the base first, he or she scores.

Noncompetitive outdoor activities are organized for children and adults with disabilities by St. David's Wheelchair Fitness Center (867-5141) or the city's Parks and Recreation Department. PARD operates the McBeth Recreation Center (327-6498 or TDD: 327-6662). Activities at the center, a totally accessible facility, include walks, dance, wheelchair sports, and camp programs. Located at 2401-A Columbus Drive, the center can be reached from the southwest end of Zilker Park where the frontage road of MoPac intersects Columbus Drive.

Therapeutic Recreation Outreach (480-3011), at 901 West Riverside Drive, sponsors Special Olympics and organizes a canoeing and kayaking clinic for people with disabilities every summer at **Fiesta Gardens**. Other programs of Therapeutic Recreation Outreach feature cycling, golfing, gardening, camping, and an award-winning adapted aquatics program that includes parasailing and water skiing.

Therapeutic Recreation Outreach offers horseback riding that accommodates people with disabilities. Another possibility is the **Cameron Equestrian Center** (272-4301) in northeast Austin, where a certified instructor for children with special needs ensures a quality program for handicapped riders.

For people with disabilities, riding affords an excellent opportunity to develop physical fitness outdoors. While many stables accommodate for disabilities, one outstanding program is the Handicapped Equestrian Learning Program (HELP). A volunteer organization operating on private land, HELP provides carefully monitored riding opportunities for even severely disabled people. Families working together to maintain the program report success in the development of muscular fitness and self-esteem, not to mention the enjoyment of the outdoors. Write HELP at 2908 Gregg Lane, Manor, Texas, 78653, or call 251-1099 for more information. Volunteers will be glad to help you.

Although hike-and-bike trails are not paved, many of them are flat enough to make wheelchair mobility feasible. Places to consider include the **Town Lake Hike-and-Bike Trail**, and some—but not all—of the trails around the **Austin Nature Center**, **Mayfield Park** at the west end of 35th Street, and **Stacy Park** in south central Austin. On the northeast end of town, the **Jourdan-Bachman Pioneer Farm** might be another option. Look for accessibility signs.

A fairly new metropolitan park nearly the size of Zilker is **Mary Moore Searight Park** in far south Austin at 907 Slaughter Lane. The trail system at this multifunctional facility includes a jogging trail, an equestrian trail, and a paved trail suitable for wheelchairs. Although the main entrance to Mary Moore Searight Park is on Slaughter Lane, the easiest way to the paved trail is to turn off Slaughter Lane at Bilbrook Place where you will see a sign to the Texas Oaks subdivision. Take Bilbrook south to Watchful Fox Road and turn right. After a few blocks, turn left onto Decker Prairie Drive, which deadends at the southwest end of the park. Look for the plaque labeled "Slaughter Creek District Park," on which a map shows the paved trail leading to Slaughter Creek.

Slaughter Creek District Park is not a separate park, but it has a distinct name perhaps because the land that comprises Mary Moore Searight Park was acquired gradually in 3 parcels of 50 acres, 88 acres, and 206 acres, for a total of 344. Park hours are 5 a.m. to 10 p.m.

A new park in southwest Austin, **Dick Nichols District Park**, has been designed with a multipurpose trail, interactive playscape, and other outdoor amenities. To reach the park, take MoPac south, go west on William Cannon, and turn south on Beckett Road. The park is off Beckett Road.

Dirt trails through **Blunn Creek Nature Preserve,** north of St. Edward's University, make most of the preserve unsuitable for people with mobility impairments, but there is a short trail at the northeast end that is smooth. The view of "Old Main," as the prominent building at St. Edward's University is affectionately called, is sure to instill that wonderful feeling of being outdoors. From IH 35, turn west onto Oltorf, where Travis High School is on the corner. The point of access is behind the school along the west side of the campus.

Where Ben White ends and Loop 360 begins, there is a point of access to the **Barton Creek Greenbelt** on the north side of Loop 360. There is a wheelchair symbol there, but the trail is fairly rugged and disappointingly short. Farther north on Loop 360, on the east side, is the **Wild Basin Wilderness Preserve** (327-7622), which has an unpaved trail about a third of a mile long that bears a wheelchair symbol. Caution is also in order here, however, because of some of the inclines. (See Chapter 2, *At the Park*, for more information on Wild Basin Wilderness Preserve.)

One of the best parks for wheelchairs or other mobility impairments is **McKinney Falls State Park** (243-1643), 15 miles southeast of Austin at 7102 Scenic Loop Road. The park has paved trails in a 3-mile hike-and-bike loop along Onion Creek, and there are picnic tables along the way. There is also a more rugged trail designed for a self-guided tour with the help of a pamphlet from the visitors center. For those who do not wish to venture far, there are nice exhibits inside the visitor's center and waterfalls behind it. In the spring McKinney Falls State Park hosts a weekend called Wildflower Days, when more activities than usual are available for enjoying the park. To reach the park from the east, take U.S. Highway 183 south past Texas Highway 71 and Onion Creek and turn west on Scenic Loop, where a sign points the way to the park. It is more complicated to reach the park from the west, but take IH 35 south, take the William Cannon Exit, head east, and follow a map to Scenic Loop Road.

The Austin Regional Group of the Sierra Club developed a special outings program in 1985 under the auspices of a national program called Inner City Outings (ICO). The Austin ICO program, plans an outing with a particular type of group in mind, usually in collaboration with a school or service agency, such as the Center for Attitudinal Healing, the Mary Lee Foundation, Austin State School, or a senior activity center. In the past ICO volunteers have organized outings for high school students, elderly people, state school residents, and people in wheelchairs. Information about ICO can be obtained at the Sierra Club's general meeting on the first Tuesday of each month (see *About the Sierra Club* at the back of this book).

Austin's transportation system is Capital Metro (474-1200), which provides a fixed route system that is fully accessible. You may also qualify for the services of the Special Transit System (478-9647).

PUBLICATIONS

Roth, Wendy, and Michael Tompane. *Easy Access to National Parks*. San Francisco, California: Sierra Club Books, 1992. A Sierra Club guide for people with disabilities that is also useful for senior citizens and families with young children.

Texas State Park Facilities Accessible to and Usable by the Handicapped. Texas Parks and Wildlife Department brochure. Write TPWD, 4200 Smith School Road, Austin, Texas, 78744.

■ Senior Citizens

Senior citizens can enjoy the resources in and around Austin that have already been described, so only a few sites are designed with seniors 50 years of age and older specifically in mind. The city's Parks and Recreation Department provides programs for this age group primarily at 3 senior activity centers:

- Conley-Guerrero Senior Center (478-7695)
  808 Nile Street (east)

- Senior Activity Center (474-5921)
  2874 Shoalcrest (west)

- Nueces Senior Center (476-5218)
  1506 Nueces Street (downtown)

Although many of the activities at these centers are indoors, outdoor activities can include tours, special events, and occasionally sports. One particularly big sporting event held each May is Austin Area Senior Games. People 55 and older can participate in running, cycling, swimming, golf, and tennis as part of this event. Austin frequently holds 5K or 10K races that designate winners in various age groups. In general, the city's 14 recreation centers offer a balanced menu of activities, some for all ages and others for specific age groups, including senior citizens. Residents and visitors alike are encouraged to obtain booklets, brochures, maps, and other materials produced by the Parks and Recreation Department to inform the public of the many programs it provides to all citizens.

Elderhostel is a national educational and service organization for those of us who are 55 years old or older and their spouses. It has ties to universities here and overseas, including the University of Texas. Catalogs and program information are available at the library or by writing to: Elderhostel, 75 Federal Street, Boston, Massachusetts, 02110-1941.

OUT FOR THE VIEW

9

The Highland Lakes and the diversity in topography between the Balcones Escarpment and the Blackland Prairie afford many scenic drives and views in and around Austin. A good place to start is the **State Capitol,** north of the Colorado River. There are many nice views of the Capitol from IH 35, Loop 360, and MoPac, but to see one of the best, drive north up Congress Avenue from Town Lake and look ahead at the Capitol at the end of the street.

South of Town Lake is **Zilker Park,** on Barton Springs Road, where a shelter within the **Taniguchi Oriental Garden** offers one of the nicest views in the city. Nearby within the park, **Lou Neff Point**, where Barton Creek flows into the Colorado River, is a great place to see downtown Austin up close and watch the river flow through town. Take a few minutes and relax here. On the opposite shore is another nice spot providing a view up Barton Creek. You can park on the north side of Cesar Chavez Street and walk under a bridge to get to this spot along the Zilker Hike-and-Bike Trail. During the Christmas holiday season, the lighted Christmas tree in Zilker Park can be spotted from many vantage points along MoPac or Loop 360.

Zilker Nature Preserve is located on Stratford Drive. (Stratford Drive turns off Barton Springs Road within Zilker Park.) The Austin Nature Center office will provide you with a trail map; on this map you can locate a great overlook. The start of the trail to the **Zilker Preserves Overlook** begins on Stratford Drive near Barton Springs Road. Another way to reach this overlook is to drive west on Barton Springs Road, go underneath the MoPac overpass and turn right on Rollingwood Drive. You will see a sign on your right indicating "Trail Access." Drive on to the end of the road and park in the **Zilker Club House** parking lot. Walk back to the trail; the overlook is very near the road and provides a great view of the park and preserves. The patio at the Zilker Club House also affords a nice view of the area.

The **French Legation**—the only building in Texas erected by a foreign government—charges a fee to enter the grounds but offers some nice views of downtown Austin. From IH 35 go east on 8th Street and take the first road to the left, which is Embassy Street. The entrance is to your left. As you leave the Embassy, continue north on Embassy Street, turn right onto 9th Street, and turn left at the next street, which is San Marcos. The **Ebenezer Baptist Church**, at the corner of San Marcos and 10th Street, also affords nice views of downtown Austin. As you leave Ebenezer Baptist Church, go east on 10th Street, turn right onto Waller Street, and continue until you reach 7th Street. Turn left there and continue to **Huston-Tillotson College**, which will be on your left about 3/4 of a mile down 7th Street. Turn left onto Chicon and enter the campus through the gate on the left. You will receive a great welcome from the guard, who can advise you where the best views are of downtown and east Austin from the campus area.

Going south on IH 35, turn east on Texas Highway 71 (Ben White), continue to Montopolis Drive, and turn left. Watch for **Grove Street,** which will veer off to the left (northwest). You will see a nice view of downtown as you drive down Grove, and when you reach Riverside turn right. After a long block, take another right onto Montopolis, follow Montopolis back to Ben White, turn left there, drive to Riverside, and turn left again. The intersection of **Ben White and Riverside Drive** offers another nice view of downtown and south Austin. Continuing on Riverside will bring you back into the city.

City Park Road provides magnificent views. Drive west on RM 2222, go past Loop 360, and turn left on City Park Road. You will drive along a ridge where you see the city on one side and glimpses of the Hill Country on the other. The road ends at **Emma Long Metropolitan Park** on the banks of Lake Austin.

Among the best spots for viewing the Austin skyline are Mary Moody Northern Theater and other locations on the campus of **St. Edward's University**, at 3001 South Congress Avenue. Another good spot is the **overlook on the east side of Loop 360** about 1.8 miles north of the Bee Caves Road cutoff. Also on the east side of Loop 360, 1.5 miles north of the Bee Caves Road cutoff, you will see the sign for the **Wild Basin Preserve**. A visitor's center there is staffed daily from 9 a.m. to 5 p.m., and from the porch of the visitor's center you have a nice view of the Hill Country. A short walk down the Easy Access Trail will take you to an overlook with a great view of downtown Austin. This trail, designed to accommodate mobility impairments, is ideal for a less-than-strenuous walk.

If you continue north on Loop 360 from Wild Basin, you will encounter more nice views just driving along. If you go south on Loop 360, however, turn east on Bee Caves Road, and take the second road to your left, which is **Red Bud Trail**. At the corner of Red Bud

Trail and Forest View Drive, you will encounter another outstanding view of downtown Austin. At the next crossroad, which is Lake Austin Boulevard, turn right and continue under MoPac, taking Cesar Chavez. Drive along the north side of Town Lake, continue to Congress Avenue, turn left there, and drive up **Congress Avenue** to see a favorite view of the Capitol of Texas.

Mount Bonnell is famous for its panoramic view 785 feet high above downtown and Lake Austin. This is a great place to picnic. Go west on 35th Street, veer left on Old Bull Creek Road, and turn right on Mt. Bonnell Road. Mt. Bonnell will be on your left at the top of 100 stone steps. A curfew extends from 9 p.m. to 4 a.m. As you leave Mt. Bonnell go north on Mt. Bonnell Road, turn right on Mt. Bonnell Drive, turn left on Balcones Drive, take another left onto Perry Lane, and turn left again onto Ridge Oak. Here you will find a small **hilltop park** built above a city water reservoir that offers dramatic views of the Loop 360 bridge, Austin Country Club, Lake Austin Peninsula, and Cat Mountain.

To watch the moonrise or sunset or to take pictures of the Austin skyline, drive out to **Barton Creek Square Mall** at 2901 Capital of Texas Highway (Loop 360), where Loop 360 intersects MoPac. The northeast parking lot has been outfitted for moon gazers, complete with trash receptacles and a bench. Still, watch out for the red ants if you're sitting on the grass. Also watch the sunset from the parking lot of **St. Luke's on the Lake**, a church overlooking Lake Travis with some of the best lake views. Please park in the lot west of the church and as a common courtesy don't leave your trash. The church is on RM 620 just north of Mansfield Dam.

In the **Blunn Creek Nature Preserve** a short trail at the northeast end, designed with wheelchair accessibility in mind, affords a superb view of St. Edward's University. On the south side of Oltorf Street near the intersection of IH 35, Travis High School has access to this trail along the west side of its campus.

For the best views while dining, try the **Foothills at the Hyatt Regency** at 208 Barton Springs Road on Town Lake, the **County Line** at 6500 West Bee Caves Road, or the **Oasis Cantina Del Lago** on Lake Travis. At the Oasis you can watch the nightly sunset inside through glass windows or outside year-round from decks at several levels. To get there, drive out RM 2222, take RM 620 west, turn right onto Comanche Trail, and follow the signs.

153

For great views farther out, drive northwest to any of the **High-land Lakes**, a chain of lakes 150 miles long formed by a series of dams on the Colorado River. Closest in is Austin's Town Lake, followed by lakes Austin, Travis, Marble Falls, LBJ, Inks, and Buchanan. Lake Buchanan, farthest out, is the largest of all these lakes, all of which offer recreational opportunities, such as swimming, boating, or hiking.

A scenic route to the lakes is to drive north of Austin on U.S. Highway 183, go west on RM 1431. This route will give you views of Lake Travis, Lake Marble Falls, and Lake Lyndon B. Johnson. You will pass through the town of Marble Falls. RM 1431 ends at Texas Highway 29; turn right here. After several miles Lake Buchanan and Lake Buchanan Dam will be on your left and Inks Lake will be on your right. Take Park Road 4 (turn right) at Inks Lake and continue to U.S. Highway 281. Turn right and you will be back on RM 1431 at Marble Falls after about 8 miles.

For a **scenic drive west of Austin**, go west on Texas Highway 71, continue past the turnoff for RM 620 for another couple of hundred yards, and then turn left on **Hamilton Pool Road** (RM 3238). After a few miles this road loses its status as a ranch road, becoming narrower, windier, and slightly rougher at this point. About 14.5 miles from the cutoff you will reach Hamilton Pool, named for a natural pool within a cave where a waterfall 65 feet high furnishes a constant supply of water. Shortly past the Hamilton Pool turnoff you will plunge into the Pedernales River valley. The road takes a hairpin course down and across the narrow one-lane low-water bridge, so take it easy and enjoy the scenery.

You may wish instead to drive west on U.S. Highway 290, turn right on U.S. Highway 281, pass through Johnson City on U.S. Highway 281, turn left onto RM 1323, and continue to **Willow City**. At a T-intersection where a small wooden sign says "Willow City Loop," turn left here to drive one of the most wildly beautiful roads in Texas. After about 14 miles, turn left onto Texas Highway 16. Soon you will come to Eckert, where you take a right turn and continue to the intersection of RM 965 toward **Enchanted Rock State Natural Area**. Enchanted Rock and its smaller companions are awesome. A mile-long climb to the summit will provide you with some of the best panoramic views, sunrises, and sunsets. Incidentally, Texas Highway 16 is beautiful all the way from Kerrville, southwest of Enchanted Rock, to Llano.

To take a **scenic drive south of Austin**, go south on Manchaca Road until it ends at FM 1626, where you turn right. For the next 4.5 miles you drive on the edge of the Balcones Escarpment. Bear west toward Driftwood on FM 967. When FM 967 comes to an end after 9.2 miles, turn left onto RM 1826 going west for just over a mile, and turn left on FM 150. Continue to the intersection of FM 150 and FM 3237, turn right on FM 3237, and continue to **Wimberley**. A quick way to return to Austin is to turn right on RM 12, which will take you to the town of Dripping Springs and U.S. Highway 290, where you turn right and continue east to Austin.

Or drive south on IH 35 to San Marcos and take RM 12 west. About 10 miles out of town, RM 12 suddenly veers north to Wimberley. You continue straight on RM 32. In less than 5 miles you begin to climb **Devil's Backbone**, a long and rugged hill that helps define the Guadalupe River and Blanco River watersheds. The views from the roadside park at the top are wonderful.

East of Austin, Texas Highway 71 will take you to Bastrop. Drive through Bastrop and take Texas Highway 21 north (turn left); about 1 mile east you will come to **Bastrop State Park**. Park Road 1 connects Bastrop State Park to **Buescher State Park**. There is a stop between these parks that will give you great views of the area. Both of these parks are located in the Lost Pines.

Different wildflowers bloom in different seasons. For more information see the section in this book on wildflowers. Also check the newspapers or call the **Wildflower Hotline**, 832-4059 ext. 4, starting about the middle of March through May, to determine the best areas for wildflowers. Especially in the spring—the prime time is usually the first 2 weeks in April—the views of blooming wildflowers in the Central Texas area can be glorious.

APPENDIX 1. ABOUT THE SIERRA CLUB

This edition of *Outdoors Austin: A Sierra Club Guide* was begun to commemorate the Sierra Club's centennial. The Sierra Club was founded in 1892 in California to explore and protect the Yosemite Valley, the Sierra Nevada, and other natural resources. Today the club is an international organization with more than 600,000 members.

The Austin Regional Group is part of the Lone Star Chapter, which is part of the national organization. At the local, chapter, and national levels, the club offers both outings and opportunities to work on environmental issues. As a member of the Austin group, you receive the *Austin Sierran* from the local group 10 times a year, the *Lone Star Sierran* from the chapter 7 times a year, and the *Sierra*, the national magazine every other month.

The best way to get involved with the group is to attend an outing or meeting. General meetings are held the first Tuesday of each month at the First Unitarian Church of Austin, 4700 Grover Street. To get there either take Lamar Boulevard and turn west onto 49th Street or take Burnet Road and turn east onto 49th Street; then turn south on Grover, which dead-ends at the church.

The general meeting begins at 7:00 p.m. with announcements about events, environmental issues, or activities, the purpose of which is often to solicit volunteers to help with the work of the club or to encourage people to participate in outings or other fun activities. After the announcements, a break gives people a chance to get more information about the activities that interest them or to meet and greet until the program for the evening begins. The program is usually a slide show about nature, adventure, or a significant area anywhere in the world, often with an educational focus and always very informative. Sometimes after the meeting, people go together to a local pub. In January, it is tradition for people to bring "five favorite slides" of outdoor trips they have taken and to share the fun of these outings. Instead of the usual meeting in August, the club has a picnic a little earlier in the evening at Zilker Park.

Outings offer a wonderful opportunity to explore outdoor attractions in the Austin area or further afield, usually on weekends but occasionally on a weekday. One of the most popular outings further afield is the annual trip to Big Bend National Park over Thanksgiving weekend. At least 1 other big trip is usually taken over Memorial Day or Labor Day weekend to a place of national significance, such as Guadalupe Mountains National Park. In November, we almost always take a weekend trip to Lost Maples State Natural Area and see the spectacular fall foliage. Outings organized by the local group are open to members and nonmembers alike, but nonmembers pay a somewhat higher fee. You must be a member to participate in national outings, which are listed each year in the January issue of *Sierra*, the national magazine.

The Austin Regional Group, founded in 1968, has more than 5,000 members, some of whom have led national outings or worked on environmental issues at the national level. Run totally by volunteers, the local group, which is listed in the phone book under "Sierra Club of Austin," can provide information on joining the club. The Lone Star Chapter, also based in Austin, is listed under "Sierra Club State Conservation Office." Its phone number is 477-1729. The Chapter covers all of Texas except for 3 counties in far west Texas near El Paso. It is well known statewide for its excellent environmental work with legislators and regulatory agencies.

The Austin Group and the Lone Star Chapter receive little financial help from the national office in San Francisco. The bulk of membership dues goes to the national office to support its important national and international work. The national office address is:

Sierra Club
730 Polk Street
San Francisco, California 94109
415/ 776-2211

Appendix 2. Agencies

Listed below are agencies that offer outdoor recreation opportunities, training, or information. Many are mentioned elsewhere in the book, but they are here in one spot for easier access.

Austin Community Schools
1111 West 6th Street
Austin TX 78703
499-1744

> Austin Community Schools offer a variety of classes, including outdoor recreation. All charge a nominal fee and meet at elementary schools throughout Austin. Call the number above for a catalog.

Austin Convention and Visitor's Bureau and the
Austin Historic Landmark Commission
478-0098

> The Austin Convention and Visitor's Bureau includes 2 visitor information centers: the main one at 201 East 2nd Street (**478-0098**) at the Convention Center and the other one at Robert Mueller Airport (**480-9091**).

Austin Parks and Recreation Department
200 South Lamar Boulevard
Austin, TX 78704
499-6700

Adaptive programs	327-6498
Aquatics	476-4521
Athletics	480-3015
Austin Nature Center	327-8180
Golf and tennis	480-3020
Nature preserves	327-5437
Park police	477-9762
Park safety	499-6733
Jourdan-Bachman Pioneer Farm	837-1215
Reservations of park areas for group use	480-3036
Reservations for softball	447-0651
Therapeutic recreation	480-3011

Recreation Centers

Alamo Recreation Center	474-2806
2100 Alamo Street, Austin, TX 78722	
Austin Recreation Center	476-5662
1301 Shoal Creek Boulevard, Austin, TX 78701	
Dittmar Recreation Center	441-4777
1009 Dittmar Road, Austin, TX 78745	
Dottie Jordan Recreation Center	926-3491
2803 Loyola Lane, Austin, TX 78723	
Givens Recreation Center	928-1982
3811 East 12th Street, Austin, TX 78721	
Hancock Recreation Center	453-7765
811 East 41st Street, Austin, TX 78751	
McBeth Recreation Center	327-6498
2401-A Columbus Drive, Austin, TX 78746	
Metz/Martin Recreation Center	478-8716
2407 Canterbury Street, Austin, TX 78702	
Monotopolis Recreation Center	385-5931
1200 Monotopolis Drive, Austin, TX 78741	
Northwest Recreation Center	458-4107
2913 Northland Drive, Austin, TX 78731	
Pan American Recreation Center	476-9193
2100 East 3rd Street, Austin, TX 78702	
Parque Zaragoza Recreation Center	472-7142
741 Pedernales, Austin, TX 78702	
Rosewood Recreation Center	472-6838
2300 Rosewood Avenue, Austin, TX 78702	
South Austin Recreation Center	444-6601
1100 Cumberland Road, Austin, TX 78704	

Lower Colorado River Authority
P.O. Box 220
Austin, Texas 78767-0220
512/473-4020 (TDD)
473-3200
800/776-5272

Lakes (lake levels, etc.)	ext. 3333
LCRA Rangers (safety and accident reports)	ext. 3246
Parks information	473-4083
Public information (LCRA programs or to acquire Boating Guide)	ext. 3235

Safe Boating classes (free)	ext. 2766
Shoreline management	ext. 3217

Pflugerville Parks and Recreation Department
700 Pflugerville Loop
Pflugerville, TX 78664
251-5082

Park reservations	251-5082
Swimming Pool	251-5082

Round Rock Parks and Recreation Department
605 Palm Valley Boulevard
Round Rock, TX 78664
218-5540

Information Line	867-6442
Swimming Pool/Lake Creek Park	255-0342

Texas Department of Transportation
Travel and Information Division
P.O. Box 5064
Austin, TX 78763
800/452-9292 (8 a.m. to 9 p.m. central time)

The Texas Department of Transportation publishes the award-winning magazine *Texas Highways* and the state's tourist literature, available free from the address given above. Particularly recommended are the *Texas Events Calendar*, published 4 times a year and *Texas*, a thick, colorful guide to all the state's major attractions. TXDOT also operates 11 Travel Information Centers to provide the public with information on points of interest, attractions, recreation areas, and routes. The Travel Information Center in Austin is housed at the Capitol Complex Visitor's Center (**463-8586**).

Texas Parks and Wildlife Department
4200 Smith School Road
Austin, TX 78744
389-8950
800/792-1112 (for information only)

Besides managing state parks, natural areas, and historic sites, TPWD publishes the monthly magazine *Texas Parks and Wildlife* and offers an award-winning environmental education program called Project Wild. An outreach program, Project Wild travels to Texas schools and other locations to conduct workshops for teachers. Call for a list of upcoming workshops throughout the state. To make reservations at state parks, call **512/389-8900** or write: TPWD Reservation Center, P. O. Box 17488, Austin, Texas, 78760-7488. To subscribe to *Texas Parks and Wildlife* call **800/937-9393** during regular business hours.

Travis County Parks, Visitor Information and Reservations
473-9437

Hamilton Pool Preserve	264-2740
Pace Bend Park	264-1482
Park Rangers	266-3315
Emergency After Hours	473-9285

University of Texas Informal Classes
2323 San Antonio Street Suite A
Austin TX 78705
(512)471-0975

Informal Classes cover a wide variety of topics, including outdoor activities. All are noncredit and require a fee (higher for non-UT folks). There are several sessions a year, and the current or next listing is readily available.

U.S. Fish and Wildlife Service
611 East 6th Street
Austin TX 78701
482-5436

Balcones National Wildlife Refuge-Realty	482-5700
Ecological Service Division	482-5436
National Fish Hatchery and Technology Center	
San Marcos, TX	Austin telephone number: 482-5810
Geological Survey/Water Resources Division	873-3000

UT Recreational Sports Outdoor Program   471-1093

UT rec sports, as it is usually called, offers programs for both students and nonstudents. The Outdoor Program (**471-1093**) schedules trips not only close to home but also far from Austin.

Appendix 3. Maps

The maps listed below are helpful or unusual but not necessarily easy to obtain. Some are subject to limited printing. It may be necessary to contact the map publisher or search the library.

A.I.D. Associates. *Guadalupe River: Canyon Dam to New Braunfels, Texas*. Irving, Texas: A.I.D. Associates, 1987. Colorful map that warns of dangerous spots for canoers.

Austin Parks and Recreation Department. *City of Austin Map and Facilities Guide*. Colorado Springs, CO: american MAP advertising co., 1994. Shows where parks are located throughout Austin with matrix on the back of the map giving detailed information about facilities at each park. Also features a nice map of Town Lake.

Coggeshall Map Service. *San Marcos and New Braunfels, Texas*. Harlingen, Texas: Coggeshall Map Service. Labeled a Rand McNally map on the front, this map shows San Marcos on one side and New Braunfels on the other.

Graphic Maps. *City of Austin Pocket Map*. Houston, Texas: Graphic Maps, 1992. Similar to *Austin: An Unusual Map of the Capitol of Texas* described below, this map is good for newcomers who want to see the downtown parks and points of interest. It has special maps of Lake Travis, the corridor between Austin and San Antonio, and the entire state of Texas.

Lower Colorado River Authority. *Colorado River Trail Explorer's Map*. Austin, Texas: Lower Colorado River Authority. Shows the Colorado River stretching from west to east in the 10 counties of San Saba, Llano, Burnet, Blanco, Travis, Bastrop, Fayette, Colorado, Wharton, and Matagorda. The back side of the map shows points of interest in each of these counties.

Lower Colorado River Authority. *Highland Lakes Camping and Boating Guide*. Austin, Texas: Lower Colorado River Authority. Shows parks and recreation areas along the 7 Highland Lakes: Lake Buchanan, Inks Lake, Lake Lyndon B. Johnson, Lake Marble Falls, Lake Travis, Lake Austin, and Town Lake.

Lower Colorado River Authority. *Lake Travis Boating Guide*. Austin, Texas: Lower Colorado River Authority and KVUE 24. Stretches from the west end at Lake Marble Falls and Max Starke Dam to the east end at Mansfield Dam Recreation Area. A chart tells what facilities are available at 7 LCRA parks (operated by Travis County): Arkansas Bend, Cypress Creek, Hippie Hollow, Mansfield Dam, Pace Bend, Sandy Creek, and Windy Point. Shows where these sites and 31 marinas are located along Lake Travis.

Map Ventures. *South Central Texas*. Pflugerville, Texas: Map Ventures, 1993. Recommended for use with this book because it covers the same area as the book and highlights many of the same features.

McLeod, Gerald E. and Tim Grisham. "Barton Creek Guide." *Austin Chronicle*. Excellent guide to Barton Creek.

National Off-Road Bicycle Association. *Barton Creek Greenbelt Trail Map: Loop 360 to Zilker Park*. Manchaca, Texas: Breakthrough Publications, 1988. A laminated map intended for off-road bicyclers but useful for others as well.

Old San Francisco Steak House Development Corporation. *Austin: An Unusual Map of the Capitol of Texas*, Texas Commemorative Edition. Austin, Texas: Old San Francisco Steak House Development Corporation, 1987. Shows the Austin Nature Center, Barton Springs, Wild Basin Wilderness Preserve, Mt. Bonnell, Mansfield Dam, and several parks, including Lake Austin Metropolitan Park and Zilker Park. Also shows the major buildings and features of Austin, including St. Edward's University, UT tower and campus, Camp Mabry, and Laguna Gloria Art Museum.

Rand McNally. *Highland Lakes of Central Texas*. Chicago, Illinois: Rand McNally, 1989. Shows parks, recreation areas, and streets along Lake Buchanan, Inks Lake, Lake Lyndon B. Johnson, Lake Marble Falls, Lake Travis (including LCRA's Pace Bend Recreation Area), and Lake Austin but not Town Lake.

Rand McNally. *Round Rock, Georgetown, Leander, and Cedar Park, Texas*. Chicago, Illinois: Rand McNally, 1990. Shows Lake Georgetown and a special map of Travis County and the surrounding area.

Shearer Publishing. *The Roads of Texas*. Fredericksburg, Texas:
Shearer Publishing, 1988. This atlas is extremely useful for traveling the backroads of Texas, and it shows the major roads and
highways as well. Especially useful is a chart showing the facilities
available at all state parks, state recreation areas, state historical
parks, state natural areas, and national parks and forests. A wealth
of unusual information, the atlas also includes descriptions of forts
and missions, ghost towns, roadside attractions, and festivals and
annual events.

Texas Parks and Wildlife Department.*Texas State Parks*. Austin,
Texas: Texas Parks and Wildlife Department, 1994. Shows all the
state parks, state historical parks, state natural areas, and partner-
ship parks in Texas. A large matrix gives the phone number, facilities, and special features for each site. Other information includes
fees, park passports, and how to make reservations. To obtain this
brochure free of charge call 800/792-1112.

Texas Department of Transportation. Series of county maps. A map
of every county in Texas is available in three sizes from the Texas
Department of Transportation. TXDOT maintains a Map Sales
office at Jackson and 40th Streets, east of MoPac Boulevard across
from Camp Mabry. Map Sales is housed in Building 2 and open
8 a.m. to 5 p.m. Monday through Friday.

Treaty Oak Press. *Austin Old and New*. Austin, Texas: Treaty Oak
Press, 1984. Centers on the sites in downtown Austin and the
University of Texas campus, giving historical information on these
sites on the back side of the map. Special features include a brief
history of early Austin and a museum directory.

Appendix 4. Publications

Below are some helpful publications about Austin and nonmotorized, non-team sport outdoor recreation.

Austin. 3rd ed. Houston: Gulf Publishing, 1992. Other Texas Monthly Guidebooks on Texas include *Hill Country, San Antonio, Texas, Texas Bed and Breakfast,* and *Texas Parks and Campgrounds.*

Austin Environmental Handbook, Austin, Texas: Ecology Action. Published every year.

Ganci, Dave. *Hiking the Southwest.* San Francisco, California: Sierra Club Books, 1992. This Sierra Club Totebook covers Arizona, New Mexico, and West Texas. Other Sierra Club Totebooks include *The Best of Backpacking, Fieldbook of Nature Photography*, and *Outing Leader's Handbook.*

Little, Mickey. *Camper's Guide to Texas Parks, Lakes and Forests.* Houston, Texas: Gulf Publishing, 1992. Lists camping sites within each of 4 geographical areas, with maps as well as information on facilities at each site.

————. *Hiking and Backpacking Trails of Texas.* 3rd ed. Houston, Texas: Gulf Publishing, 1990.

Miller, George O., and Delena Tull. *Texas Parks and Campgrounds.* Houston, Texas: Gulf Publishing, 1990. This is a descriptive alphabetical list of state parks and national parks and campgrounds, as well as many noncommercial and concession-operated campgrounds; does not include maps.

Permenter, Paris, and John Bigley. *Day Trips from San Antonio and Austin.* Kansas City, Missouri: Shifra Stein's Day Trips America Series, Twolane Press, 1992. Lists more than 100 day trips, most within a 2-hour drive of the city, and recommends what to see, how to get there, what hassles to avoid, where to eat, and where to stay.

Texas State Travel Guide. Austin, Texas: Texas Department of Transportation Division of Travel and Information. A thick and colorful guide provided free of charge.

Texas Highways. Austin, Texas: Texas Department of Transportation. A monthly magazine.

Texas Parks and Wildlife. Austin, Texas: Texas Parks and Wildlife Department. This monthly magazine usually includes information on specific Texas parks and on wildlife conservation.

Texas Public Campgrounds. Austin, Texas: Texas Department of Transportation Division of Travel and Information. This directory lists only facilities administered by federal, state, and local governments in Texas. For information on commercial campgrounds, contact the Texas Association of Campground Owners, 6900 Oak Leaf Drive, Orange, Texas, 77630.

This Is Austin! Austin, Texas: *Austin American-Statesman,* 1995. Contains several sections, including "Newcomers' Guide," "Environment and the Outdoors," "Recreation and Sports," and "Fiftysomethings." Published every year.

APPENDIX 5. GEOGRAPHIC LIST OF SITES

The purpose of this appendix is to provide you with a compilation of various sites in a geographical area of interest. The sites have been correlated to the sectors (Central, North, East, South, and West) and quadrants (Northeast, Northwest, Southwest, and Southeast) discussed in the introduction. The sites are in alphabetical order within sector or quadrant. Sites are managed by the Austin Parks and Recreation Department (PARD) unless otherwise specified.

Either an address or directions to the facility are included. Phone numbers are listed when a phone is on-site; otherwise the site does not have its own phone or the site is not listed in the Austin phone book. Sites mentioned in this book are noted with an asterisk (*) after the site name. Page numbers of site references are in the index. This appendix was derived from information available through

- Austin Parks and Recreation Department (PARD)
- Travis County Parks
- LCRA Parks
- Texas Parks and Wildlife Department

Central Sector

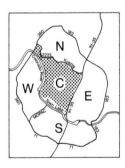

(Bounded by RM 2222, IH 35, the Colorado River, and a short stretch of Loop 360)

Adams-Hemphill Park
3001 Hemphill Park

Austin High Tennis Center
2001 West 1st Street
477-7802

Austin Recreation Center (*)
1301 Shoal Creek Boulevard
476-5662

Bailey Park
1101 West 33rd Street

Barton Creek Greenbelt (*)
Zilker Park to Loop 360 to Lost Creek Subdivision

Brush Square (*)
401 East 5th Street

Camp Mabry (*)
35th Street just west of MoPac

Caswell Tennis Center
2312 Shoal Creek Boulevard
478-6268

Clarksville Park
1811 West 11th Street

Deep Eddy Pool (*)
Next to Eilers Park
401 Deep Eddy Avenue
472-8546

Duncan Park (*)
10th Street at Shoal Creek

Eastwoods Park
3001 Harris Park Boulevard

Eilers Park (*)
(see Deep Eddy Pool)

Elisabet Ney Museum
304 East 44th Street
458-2255

Hancock Golf Course
811 East 41st Street
453-0276

Hancock Recreation Center
811 East 41st Street
453-7765

Johnson Creek Greenbelt (*)
Enfield Road to Town Lake

Laguna Gloria (*)
3809 West 35th Street
458-8191

Lamar Beach
(Town Lake Metropolitan Park)
Lamar Boulevard to Eilers Park

Lions Municipal Golf Course
2901 Enfield Road
477-6963

Mayfield House
3801 Old Bull Creek Road
453-7236

Mayfield Preserve (*)
3505 West 35th Street
452-7236

Mt. Bonnell Park (*)
3800 Mt. Bonnell Road

Northwest Recreation Center
2913 Northland Drive
458-4107

Nueces Senior Center (*)
1506 Nueces Street
476-5218

O'Henry Museum (*)
409 East 5th Street
472-1903

OId Bakery and Emporium
1006 Congress Avenue
477-5961

Palm Park
200 North IH 35

Pease District Park (*)
1100 Kingsbury Street

Perry Park
4900 Fairview Drive

Ramsey Park
4301 Rosedale Avenue

Red Bud Isle (*)
(Town Lake Metropolitan Park)
3401 Red Bud Trail

Reed Park
2600 Pecos Street

Republic Square
422 Guadalupe Street

Seider Springs Park (*)
(Shoal Creek Greenbelt)
1320 West 34th Street

Senior Activity Center (*)
2874 Shoal Crest Avenue
474-5921

Shipe Park
4400 Avenue G

Shoal Creek Greenbelt (*)
Town Lake to 38th Street

Symphony Square (*)
1101 Red River Street
(11th and Red River)

Tarrytown Park
2106 Tower Drive

Texas Memorial Stadium (*)
UT campus on Red River Street

Town Lake (*)
Colorado River from Tom Miller
Dam on the west to Colorado
River Park on the east

Town Lake Hike-and-Bike
Trail (*)
(see Town Lake)

Town Lake Metropolitan
Park (*)
Colorado River from Tom Miller
Dam on the west to Colorado
River Park on the east
462-2677

Treaty Oak Park (*)
503 Baylor Street

Waller Creek Greenbelt (*)
15th Street to Town Lake

Walsh Boat Landing
1600 Scenic Drive

Waterloo Park (*)
403 East 15th Street

West Austin Park
1317 West 10th Street

Westenfield Park
2008 Enfield Road

Williams Field
Town Lake at North Lamar
Boulevard
Near YMCA

Wooldridge Square (*)
900 Guadalupe Street

North Sector

(Bounded by Loop 360, Highway 183, IH 35, an RM2222)

Allen Park (*)
Travis County/LCRA
on Westside Drive
Near Mopac and Hart Lane

Barrow Preserve (*)
7715 Long Point Drive
327-5437

Brentwood Park
6710 Arroyo Seca

Bull Creek District Park (*)
6700 Lakewood Drive

Bull Creek Greenbelt (*)
Loop 360 to Bull Creek to
Spicewood Springs Road

Doss Playground
7005 Northledge Drive

Gullett Playground
6310 Treadwell Boulevard

Hill Playground
8601 Tallwood Drive

Lucy Read Playground
2608 Richcreek Road

Murchison Pool
3700 North Hills Drive

Northwest District Park (*)
7000 Ardath Street
453-0194

Pillow Playground
3025 Crosscreek Drive

Reilly Playground
405 Denson Drive

Steck Valley Greenbelt
Between Loop 360 and end of
Steck Avenue

T.A. Brown Park
505 West Anderson Lane

Wooten Park (*)
1406 Dale Drive

East Sector

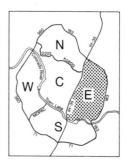

(Bounded by IH 35, Highway 183, and the Colorado River)

Alamo Park and Recreation
Center
2100 Alamo Street
474-2806

Andrews Playground
6801 Northeast Drive

Bartholomew District Park (*)
1800 East 51st Street
928-0014

Boggy Creek Greenbelt (*)
12th Street to Webberville Road

Brooke Playground
3100 East 4th Street

Buttermilk Branch Greenbelt
7500 Meador Avenue to 7500
Providence Avenue

Carver Museum
1161 Angelina
472-4809

Colony Park
East on Decker Lake Road
between Highway 183 and
FM 3177, before
Walter E. Long Lake

Comal Park
300 Comal Street

Conley-Guerrero Senior Activity
Center (*)
808 Nile Street
478-7695

Dottie Jordan Park and
Recreation Center (*)
2803 Loyola Lane
926-3491

Downs/Mabson Fields (*)
2812 East 12th Street
499-6749

Festival Beach (*)
(Town Lake Metropolitan Park)
IH 35 North eastward to
Canadian Street

Fiesta Gardens (*)
(Town Lake Metropolitan Park)
2101 Bergman Avenue

French Legation Museum
802 San Marcos Street
472-8180

Givens District Park and
Recreation Center (*)
3911 East 12th Street
928-1982

Govalle Park
5200 Bolm Road

J.J.Seabrook Greenbelt
East on FM 969 past Airport
Boulevard but before Morris
Williams Golf Course

Kealing Playground
Near intersection of Rosewood
and Comal Street

Lott Park
1180 Curve Street

Martin Park
1601 Haskell Street

Metz Park and Recreation
Center (*)
2407 Canterbury Street
478-8716

Morris Williams Golf Course
4305 Manor Road
926-1298

Norman Playground
4101 Tannehill Lane

Oak Springs Playground
3601 Webberville Road

Ortega Playground
1135 Garland Avenue

Pan Am Park and Recreation
Center
2100 East 3rd Street
476-9193

Parque Zaragoza Recreation
Center (*)
741 Pedernales Street
472-7142

Patterson Park
4200 Brookview Road

Pecan Springs Playground
3100 Rogge Lane

Pharr Tennis Center
4201 Brookview Road
477-7773

Rebekah Baines Johnson
North Town Lake, east of IH 35

Rosewood Park and
Recreation Center (*)
1182 North Pleasant Valley
Road
472-6838

Sanchez Playground
North of Haskell, east of IH 35

Springdale Park
Off of Webberville Road

St. Johns Park
910 East St. Johns

Zaragoza
See Parque Zaragosa Recreation Center

South Sector

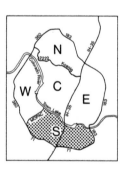

*(Bounded by the Colorado
River, Highway 183, Ben
White Boulevard / Texas
Highway 71 and MoPac)*

Airman's Cave
Entrance on Barton Creek
about 0.75 miles down-
stream from Loop 360 bridge
over the creek

Auditorium Shores (*)
(Town Lake Metropolitan Park)
Lamar Boulevard to South 1st
Street

Austin Area Garden Center (*)
2220 Barton Springs Road
477-8672

Austin Nature Center (*)
301 Nature Center Drive
327-8180

Austin Parks and Recreation
Department (*)
Administrative Offices
200 South Lamar Boulevard
499-6700

Barton Creek Greenbelt (*)
Zilker Park to South Loop 360
to Lost Creek subdivision

Barton Hills Playground
2108 Barton Hills Drive

Barton Springs Pool (*)
(Zilker Metropolitan Park)
2131 William Barton Drive
476-9044

Blunn Creek Greenbelt (*)
Along Eastside Drive in Travis
Heights

Blunn Creek Preserve (*)
1200 block of St. Edward's
Drive, Oltorf access just west of
Travis High School
327-8181

Butler Shores (*)
(Town Lake Metropolitan Park)
East bank of Barton Creek to
Lamar Bridge over Town Lake

Civitan Park
513 Vargas Road

Dougherty Cultural Arts Center
1110 Barton Springs Road
477-1371

Gillis Park
2501 South 1st Street

Mabel Davis District Park (*)
3427 Parker Lane
441-5247 (pool)

McBeth Recreation Center (*)
2502 Columbus Drive
327-6498

Montopolis Park and Recreation
Center
1200 Montopolis Drive
385-5931

Palmer Auditorium
(Town Lake Metropolitan Park)
400 South 1st Street
320-4453

Ricky Guerrero Park
2006 South 6th Street

South Austin Park and
Recreation Center (*)
1100 Cumberland Road
444-6601

South Austin Tennis Center
1000 Cumberland Road
442-1466

St. Edward's University (*)
3001 South Congress Avenue
448-8400

St. Elmo Playground
4410 South 1st Street

Stacy Park (Big) (*)
700 East Live Oak Street

Stacy Park (Little) (*)
Sunset Lane

Umlauf Sculpture Garden (*)
605 Robert E. Lee Boulevard
at Barton Springs Road

Yates Park
6200 Felix Avenue

Zachary Scott Theatre
1421 West Riverside Drive

Zilker Botanical Gardens (*)
2220 Barton Springs Road

Zilker Dinosaur Trackways (*)
2220 Barton Springs Road

Zilker Hillside Theater (*)
2201 Barton Springs Road
477-2238

Zilker Metropolitan Park (*)
(Barton Springs Pool)
2100 Barton Springs Road
472-4914

Zilker Nature Preserve
301 Nature Center Drive
327-5437
Zilker Park (*)
1900 Bluebonnet Lane

West Sector

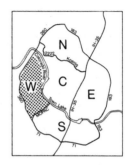

*(Bounded by MoPac, Loop 360,
and the Colorado River)*

Austin Nature Center/Zilker
Preserve (*)
301 Nature Center Drive
327-8180

Bee Creek Preserve (*)
Red Bud Trail and Forest View
Drive

Lake Austin (*)
Colorado River above Tom Miller
Dam

Vireo Preserve (*)
100 through 900 block,
Loop 360 north, east side, access
by reservation only
327-5437

Wild Basin Wilderness Preserve (*)
805 North Capital of Texas
Highway
327-7622

Zilker Preserve/Austin Nature
Center
301 Nature Center Drive
327-5437

Northeast Quadrant

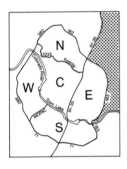

*North of the Colorado River /
East of IH 35)*

Bastrop State Park (*)
Box 518
Bastrop 78602-0518
321-2101

Big Walnut Creek Greenbelt (*)
Walnut Creek, north of Northeast District Park

Big Walnut Creek Preserve (*)
Walnut Creek, North of Northeast District Park

Buescher State Park (*)
Box 75
Smithville 78957-0075
237-2241

Hornsby Bend Wastewater
Treatment Facility
10004 Platt Lane
929-1000

Indian Grass Prairie Preserve (*)
Lindell and South Bluff
Northeast of Walter E. Long
Lake Park

Jourdan-Bachman Pioneer
Farm (*)
11418 Sprinkle Cut-off Road
837-1215

Lake Georgetown (*)
(Williamson County Park)
Georgetown, take RM 3238 Exit,
turn left, 3 miles to park entry

Lake Somerville State Park (*)
(Birch Creek unit)
Route 1, Box 499
Somerville 77879-9713
(409) 535-7763

Lake Somerville State Park (*)
(Nails Creek unit)
Route 1, Box 61C
Ledbetter 78946-9512
FM 180, 15 miles off US 290
(409) 289-2392

Lake Walter E. Long Metropolitan Park (*)
6614 Blue Bluff Road
926-5230

Manor Park
Travis County
Manor, off Carrie Manor Road at
the East Rural Community
Center

Monument Hill/Kreische
Brewery (*)
Route 1, Box 699
La Grange 78945
(409) 968-5658

Mother Neff State Park (*)
Route 1, Box 58
Moody 76557
(817) 853-2389

North Oaks Park
900 Plaza Drive

Northeast District Park (*)
5909 Coolbrook Drive

Rocky Hill Ranch (*)
Highway 71 southeast past
Bastrop, left on FM 153, past
Buescher State Park; continue
on 153 for 2 miles

Walnut Creek Metropolitan Park
North Lamar, south of Coxville
Road
834-0824

Northwest Quadrant

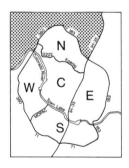

*(North of the Colorado River /
West of IH 35)*

Arkansas Bend Park (*)
LCRA Lake Travis
South on Lohmann Ford Road
from RM 1431, then 3 miles
down Sylvester Ford Road
320-7435

Balcones District Park (*)
12017 Amherst

Barrington Playground
400 Cooper Drive

Bob Wentz Park at
Windy Point (*)
LCRA Lake Travis
Comanche Trail, about 3.1
miles north of RM 620
320-7435

Bull Creek District Park (*)
Loop 360 and Lakewood Drive

Bull Creek Greenbelt (*)
Loop 360 to Bull Creek to
Spicewood Springs Road

Camp Creek Park (*)
LCRA Lake Travis (Burnet
County) About 8 miles east of
Marble Falls on RM 1431, at
end of County Road 343
473-4083

Canyon Vista Pool
8455 Spicewood Springs Road

City Park (*)
(*see* Emma Long Metropolitan
Park)

Colorado Bend State Park (*)
(Primitive area)
Box 118
Bend 76824
At Lampasas, turn left on FM
580 and continue to Bend
(915) 628-3240

Cook Playground
1511 Cripple Creek Drive

Cypress Creek Park (*)
LCRA Lake Travis
On RM 2769 at intersection of
Old Anderson Mill road about 3.4
miles west of RR 620 intersection
320-7435

Dink Pearson Park (*)
Travis County operated/LCRA
owned. On Lake Austin at end
of Lohmans Crossing Road in
Point Venture

Emma Long Metropolitan Park (*)
(aka City Park)
1600 City Park Road
346-1831

Forest Ridge Preserve
Loop 360 south of Spicewood
Springs Road
327-5437

Fritz Hughes Park (*)
Travis County operated/LCRA
owned. Lake Austin, just below
Mansfield Dam

Havins Ballfields
(Walnut Creek Metropolitan
Park)
12138 North Lamar Boulevard

Hippie Hollow (*)
(*see* McGregor Park)

Inks Lake State Park (*)
Route 2, Box 31
Burnet 78611
793-2223

Inner Space Caverns (*)
(privately owned)
IH 35 at exit 259
863-5545

Kennemer Pool
Peyton Gin Road

Lake Austin (*)
Colorado River above Tom
Miller Dam

Longhorn Cavern State Park (*)
Route 2, Box 23
Burnet 78611
756-4680

Mary Quinlan Park (*)
Travis County operated/LCRA
owned. Lake Austin at the end
of Quinlan Park Road, 5.5 miles
off RM 620

McGregor Park (*)
(*see* Hippie Hollow) LCRA
Lake Travis on Comanche Trail
about 1.6 miles north of RM 620
320-7435

Oakview Park
10800 Oak View Drive

Ron Rigsby Park
1110 Little Elm Park

Sandy Creek (*)
LCRA. Lake Travis 6 miles
southwest on Lime Creek Road
off RM 1431 about 1.8 miles west of
U.S. Highway 183 intersection
320-7435

Schroeter Park
11701 Big Trail

Selma Hughes Park (*)
Travis County operated/LCRA
owned. Lake Austin 4.5 miles
down Quinlan Park Road on
Selma Hughes Road

Tom Hughes Park (*)
Travis County operated/LCRA
owned. Lake Austin at end of
Park Drive, about 1/2 mile off
RM 620

Upper Bull Creek
District Park (*)
Loop 360 along Spicewood
Springs Road to
U.S. Highway 183
320-4453

Walnut Creek Metropolitan
Park (*)
(aka Havins Ballfields)
12138 North Lamar Boulevard

Windy Point Park
14421 Ridgetop Terrace
250-1963

Wooldridge Playground
1412 Norseman Terrace

Yett Creek Park
Off Parmer Lane

Southwest Quadrant

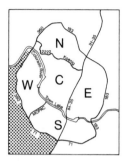

*(South of the Colorado River /
West of IH 35)*

Admiral Nimitz Museum and
Historical Center (*)
Box 777
Fredericksburg 78624
(210) 997-4379

Aquarena Springs (*)
San Marcos
Drive IH 35 south about 30
minutes, take exit 206, turn
west on Aquarena Springs
Drive, follow signs
396-8900

Battlebend Park
4700 Suburban Drive

Blanco State Park (*)
Box 493
Blanco 78606
(210) 833-4333

Camp Chautauqua (*)
LCRA
Pace Bend Recreation Area
264-1752

Cascade Caverns (*)
Boerne
(210) 755-8080

Cave without a Name (*)
(aka Century Cave)
Boerne
(210) 537-4212

Circle C Metropolitan Park (*)
Southwest Soccer Complex
Slaughter Creek and South MoPac

Commons Ford Metropolitan
Park (*)
614 Commons Ford Road North
263-5478

Cunningham Playground
2200 Berkley Avenue

Dick Nichols District Park (*)
8001 Beckett Road
Williamson Creek Greenbelt off
Beckett

Dittmar Park and Recreation
Center (*)
1009 West Dittmar Road
441-4777

Enchanted Rock State Natural
Area (*)
Route 4, Box 170
Fredericksburg 87624
(915) 247-3903

Garrison District Park (*)
6001 Manchaca Road
441-2772

Guadualupe River State Park (*)
3350 Park Road 31
Spring Branch 78070
(210) 438-2656

Hamilton Pool Preserve (*)
Take Highway 71, turn west on
Hamilton Pool Road (RM 3238):
13 miles to reach pool
264-2740

Hill Country State Natural
Area (*)
Route 1, Box 601
Bandera 78003
Take Highway 290 west, High-
way 281 south, Highway 46
west, Highway 16 west, State
Road 3240 a bit east, and State
Road 1077 south
(210) 796-4413

Honey Creek State Natural
Area (*)
(*see* Guadalupe River State
Park; within boundaries of that
park)

Joslin Park
4500 Manchaca Road

Karst Preserve
3900 Deer Lane

Kerrville-Shreiner State Park (*)
2385 Bandera Highway
Kerrville 78028
Take U.S. Highway 290 west to
Fredericksburg, turn left on
Highway 16 to Kerrville; 1 mile
past town turn left on
 Highway 173
(210) 257-5392

Krause Springs (*)
(Privately owned)
Box 114
Spicewood 78669
(210) 693-4181
Take Highway 71 west, cross
Pedernales River, go 7 miles,
right on Spur 91 at Exxon
station, go 1 mile, right on Spur
404, look for sign on left

Longview Park
7609 Longview Road

Loop 360 Park (*)
Travis County
On south shore of Lake Austin
directly under the Loop 360
bridge

Lost Maples State Natural
Area (*)
HC01, Box 156
Vanderpool 78885
(210) 966-3413

Lyndon B. Johnson National
Historic Park (*)
(Two separate units)
Box 329
Johnson City 78636
(210) 868-7128

Lyndon B. Johnson State
Historical Park (*)
(includes the Sauer-Beckmann
Farmstead)
Box 238
Stonewall 78761
(210) 644-2252

Mansfield Dam Recreation
Area (*)
LCRA, Lake Travis on RM 620
about 13.5 miles west of
U.S. Highway 183
320-7435

Mary Moore Searight Metropolitan Park (*)
907 Slaughter Lane

National Wildflower Research
Center (*)
4801 La Crosse Avenue
Austin 78739
292-4100

Natural Bridge Caverns (*)
26495 Natural Bridge Caverns
Road
Natural Bridge Caverns, TX
78266
(210) 651-6101
Take IH 35 south, exit 175, go
west on Natural Bridge Caverns Road (FM 3009) for 8 miles
to reach caverns

Oakhill Park
Boston Lane

Odom Playground
1010 Turtle Creek Boulevard
444-2472

Pace Bend Park (*)
LCRA
Lake Travis on RM 2322,
4.6 miles east of Highway 71
320-7435

Pedernales Falls State Park (*)
Route 1, Box 450
Johnson City 78636
(210) 868-7304

Sauer-Beckmann Farmstead (*)
(see Lyndon B. Johnson State
Park)

Slaughter Creek Metropolitan
Park
Entrance off MoPac, 9 miles
south of Slaughter Lane at
LaCrosse

South Boggy Creek Greenbelt (*)
Between South Congress
Avenue and IH 35 along Boggy
Creek

Southland Oaks Park
On Green Emerald (intersects
far south Brodie Lane)

Southwest Soccer Complex
(Circle C Metropolitan Park)
Slaughter Creek and South
MoPac

Veloway (*) (see Slaughter
Creek Metropolitan Park; the
veloway is part of this park)

Westcave Preserve (*)
Take Highway 71, turn onto
Hamilton Pool Road (RM 3238),
go 14 miles
264-2740

Williams Playground
Belclaire at Blue Valley Drive

Williamson Creek Greenbelt (*)
Adjacent to Dick Nichols
District Park

Windmill Run Park
Travis County
Oak Hill at end of Kirkham Cove

Southeast Quadrant

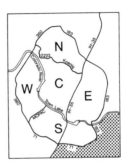

*(South of the Colorado River /
East of IH 35)*

Del Valle Softball Compound
Travis County Park
On FM 973, 4 miles south of the
U.S. Highway 183 and Highway
71 intersections

Franklin Park
4800 Copperbend Boulevard

Houston Playground
2107 Deadwood Drive

Jimmy Clay Golf Course
5400 Jimmy Clay Drive
444-0999

Little Webberville Park
Water Street
Webberville

Lockhart State Park (*)
Route 3, Box 69
Lockhart 78644-9716
398-3479

McKinney Falls State Park (*)
5808 McKinney Falls Parkway
Austin 78744
243-1643
243-0848 (Swimming Hotline)

Onion Creek District Park (*)
6900 Onion Creek Drive

Onion Creek Preserve (*)
Onion Creek, north of
Highway 71 East, access by
reservation only

Palmetto State Park (*)
Route 5, Box 201
Gonzales 78629
Take Highway 183 south 7
miles past Luling; park is off
183 on Park Road 1
(210) 672-3266

Richard Moya Park (*)
(Travis County)
Approximately 3 miles east of
Highway 183 on Burleson Road,
along Onion Creek

Webberville Park (*)
(Travis County)
3 miles east of Webberville on
FM 969

Index